"PLAIN MR WHITBREAD"

*Seven Centuries
of a Bedfordshire Family*

SAM WHITBREAD

The
Book
Castle

Sam Whitbread, born in 1937, was brought up at the family home, Southill in Bedfordshire. Educated at Eton and (briefly) Cambridge, he rejected full-time careers in politics and the family firm, preferring to concentrate on farming and forestry in Bedfordshire. He served on Bedfordshire County Council and as a Magistrate and was appointed High Sheriff in 1973. Elected to the Board of Whitbread in 1972 as a non-executive director, he became Chairman in 1984, serving for eight years at a time of great change for the Company. Sam Whitbread was appointed Lord-Lieutenant of Bedfordshire in 1991, retiring as Chairman of Whitbread the following year although remaining on the Board until 2001. He is President or Patron of a wide range of County organisations including the Bedfordshire Historical Record Society.

He is married with four children and twelve grandchildren (to whom this book is dedicated) and in 2004 handed on Southill and the Estate to his eldest son, Charles. Apart from his Lieutenancy duties, he divides his time between Bedfordshire and the Scottish Highlands. He is fond of music and watercolour painting.

First published February 2007 by
The Book Castle, 12 Church Street, Dunstable, Bedfordshire LU5 4RU
Reprinted May 2008

ISBN 978-1-903747-74-2 (hardback)
ISBN 978-1-903747-75-9 (paperback)

Designed and typeset by Caroline and Roger Hillier, The Old Chapel Graphic Design
www.theoldchapellivinghoe.com

Printed in Great Britain by Cpod, Trowbridge, Wiltshire

For my children and grandchildren

Let us now praise famous men,
and our fathers that begat us.
Ecclesiasticus xliv. 1.

People will not look forward to posterity,
who never look backward to their ancestors.
Edmund Burke
Reflections on the Revolution in France

I write books to educate myself.
Paul Johnson
Spectator, 20 September 2003

VIRTUTE NON ASTUTIA

·ARMS of WHITBREAD·

CONTENTS

List of Illustrations   vi

Foreword   vii

Chapter One **EARLY WHITBREADS**   1

Chapter Two **SAMUEL WHITBREAD I**   13

Chapter Three **SAMUEL WHITBREAD II**   27

Chapter Four **WILLIAM HENRY and SAMUEL CHARLES WHITBREAD**   45

Chapter Five **SAMUEL WHITBREAD III**   61

Chapter Six **SAMUEL HOWARD WHITBREAD**   73

Chapter Seven **SIMON WHITBREAD**   93

Afterword   106

Postscript   108

Notes on Sources   125

Index   140

ILLUSTRATIONS

Frontispiece
Coat of Arms of the Whitbreads of Southill
Granted to Samuel Howard Whitbread by the College of Arms in 1931

page x
Ion House, the Whitbreads' house in Upper Gravenhurst, by Thomas Fisher
1815–20
By kind permission of Bedfordshire & Luton Archives & Records Service

page 12
Samuel Whitbread I (1720–1796) by Sir Joshua Reynolds PRA, 1786
By kind permission of the Trustees of the Southill Chattels Trust

page 26
Samuel Whitbread II (1764–1815) by Thomas Gainsborough RA, 1788
By kind permission of the Trustees of the Southill Chattels Trust

page 44
William Henry Whitbread (1795–1867) by Sir Francis Grant RA
By kind permission of the Trustees of the Southill Chattels Trust

page 54
Samuel Charles Whitbread (1796–1879) attributed to William Bradley 1841
By kind permission of the Trustees of the Southill Chattels Trust

page 60
Samuel Whitbread III (1830–1915) by George Richmond RA, 1860
By kind permission of the Trustees of the Southill Chattels Trust

page 72
Samuel Howard Whitbread CB (1858–1944) by Sir Oswald Birley, 1930
By kind permission of Bedfordshire County Council

page 92
Simon Whitbread (1904–1985) by Edward Halliday CBE RP RBA, 1972
By kind permission of the artist's family

FOREWORD

'*E*veryone has ancestors; wherever we live, whatever our background, there is an ancestral chain stretching back into history by which we are linked to the earliest of men on earth.'

With these words I started a talk on the history of the Whitbreads which I gave to a handful of local history societies in the 1970s. I was trying to say that you don't have to be rich or famous to have ancestors; we all have them, whether we like it or not. True, there is more known about the founder of a thriving business or a leading political figure (like, in our family, the first and second Sams) than about a modest tradesman or smallholder. But, thanks to the English system of parish registers, they are all recorded, provided they were baptised, married or buried.

In the course of preparing this talk about the Whitbreads I came across information about the family that was new to me, and in recent years the idea began to grow in my mind that I ought to record as much of this information as I could, for the benefit of my children and grandchildren.

In this self-imposed task I have been greatly helped by James Collett-White who has been working on the archives at Southill for the past nine years. His long association with the Bedfordshire County Record Office (where most of the family records are deposited) has been extremely helpful and I never cease to be amazed by his extraordinarily retentive memory. However, I should make it clear that any errors of fact in this book are mine, not his. I am also lucky enough to have a daughter-in-law, Sarah, who has worked as an editor for Macmillan and Bloomsbury; her conscientious copy-editing of my manuscript showed me how much I had forgotten about punctuation since my school days!

I should like to thank Mr A G Davies (formerly of the Hertford Museum) and Robert Dimsdale for bringing to my notice the part played by my ancestor (and Robert's) in bringing down the Prime Minister Lord North in 1782.

I owe a huge debt of gratitude to Professor Richard Marks of the University of York for offering to compile the index, as well as to Paul Bowes and Sally Siddons at The Book Castle for their help and advice with the book and for their faith in its commercial possibilities.

I should also point out, lest other members of the family be offended, that the lives described in this book are of those who were my direct ancestors. I have had to omit younger brothers – and indeed sisters, some of whom married distinguished men and supported them, like Sam II's sister Emma, who married Lord St John of Bletsoe; Sam's daughter Emma Laura, wife of Charles Shaw-Lefevre, later Viscount Eversley; and Sam III's daughter, Juliana, who married Thomas Coke, later the 2nd Earl of Leicester.

I am sometimes asked why, with six Members of Parliament in the family – at least two of them highly prominent – a peerage never came our way. As we shall see, Samuel Whitbread III had two opportunities in this respect, as well as being offered a seat in the Cabinet and (twice) the Speakership of the House of Commons. His attitude, and that of his son Samuel Howard, was to 'remain plain Mr Whitbread' – hence the title of this book.

On the death of Samuel Charles Whitbread in 1879, a leading article in the *Daily News* referred to the family in these words: 'The Whitbreads in England, like the Adamsons in America, illustrate as emphatically as any of our noble houses the persistence of political talent in races and families. Connected through several generations with the aristocracy, they have never merged themselves in it. They have accepted neither peerage or title of any kind. The successive heads of the house have been simply Samuel Whitbreads. Country gentlemen by tastes and pursuits, they have maintained through their celebrated brewery a connection with trade of which there is in some minds a disposition to feel ashamed when the ladder has been climbed which it has offered to ambitious scalers of the heights of society and politics... To hold a high place and an untitled name among the commoners of England is perhaps a more legitimate subject for pride than to be the wearer of a newly-invented title and of a brand-new coronet.'

Sam Whitbread, Glebe House, Southill, Bedfordshire

THE WHITBREADS – AN OUTLINE FAMILY TREE

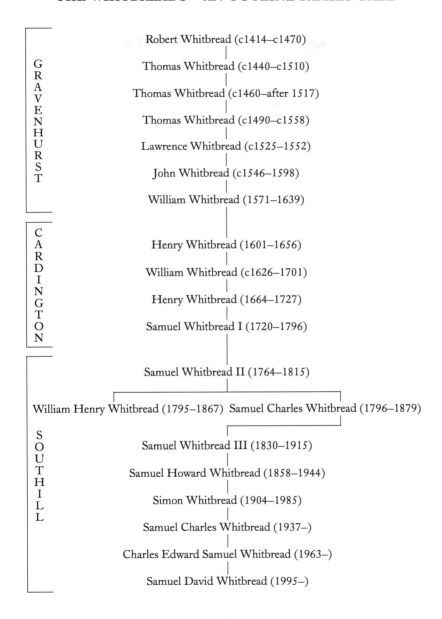

GRAVENHURST

Robert Whitbread (c1414–c1470)
|
Thomas Whitbread (c1440–c1510)
|
Thomas Whitbread (c1460–after 1517)
|
Thomas Whitbread (c1490–c1558)
|
Lawrence Whitbread (c1525–1552)
|
John Whitbread (c1546–1598)
|
William Whitbread (1571–1639)

CARDINGTON

Henry Whitbread (1601–1656)
|
William Whitbread (c1626–1701)
|
Henry Whitbread (1664–1727)
|
Samuel Whitbread I (1720–1796)
|
Samuel Whitbread II (1764–1815)

William Henry Whitbread (1795–1867)   Samuel Charles Whitbread (1796–1879)

SOUTHILL

Samuel Whitbread III (1830–1915)
|
Samuel Howard Whitbread (1858–1944)
|
Simon Whitbread (1904–1985)
|
Samuel Charles Whitbread (1937–)
|
Charles Edward Samuel Whitbread (1963–)
|
Samuel David Whitbread (1995–)

The Ion House in Upper Gravenhurst.

Ion House, the Whitbreads' house in Upper Gravenhurst, by Thomas Fisher 1815–20
By kind permission of Bedfordshire & Luton Archives & Records Service

Chapter One

EARLY WHITBREADS

(1262–1727)

*I*n Cardington church there is an eighteenth-century monument to the Whitbreads, 'who, coming into England with the Normans, settled at Ion in the parish of Upper Gravenhurst in this County of Bedford, upon an estate given them by the Conqueror...'

There is no direct evidence to substantiate this claim. However, there are in Normandy to this day families with the name Blaunpain, and in the thirteenth century there are numerous references to Blancpains and Whitbreads in and around Upper Gravenhurst; the two names appear to have been interchangeable. For example, a fine of 14 May 1262 involved 'one acre in Hamstallfurlong in Eye (Ion) next land of Roger Blauncpain'.[1] A Roger Blaunpain was a witness to various deeds between 1287 and 1305. In 1288 his name is given as Blaunpayn, otherwise it is given in the Anglicised form of Witbred, Whitbred or Withbred.

I mention these two, not to claim them as ancestors (for there is no traceable link between them and more modern Whitbreads) but to show that there is at least some substance to the claim of the family 'coming into England with the Normans'. And they were certainly at Ion by 1262. Five hundred years later, the first Samuel Whitbread was to acknowledge his supposed descent from these early English Whitbreads when he referred to Shillington (the parish in which Ion was situated) as 'the ancient place of the Whitbreads'.

It is difficult to form a firm impression of the way the medieval Whitbreads lived. From the mid-thirteenth to mid-seventeenth centuries little is recorded of them except that they witnessed deeds and grants of land and were named in rentals and leases of small areas of farmland in and around Gravenhurst.[2] We can fairly describe the Whitbreads as small peasant farmers and it is only with the death of Lawrence Whitbread in 1552 that we have any firm dates to support our history. A possible family tree would read thus:

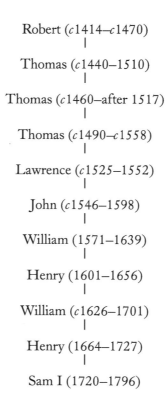

Robert (c1414–c1470)
|
Thomas (c1440–1510)
|
Thomas (c1460–after 1517)
|
Thomas (c1490–c1558)
|
Lawrence (c1525–1552)
|
John (c1546–1598)
|
William (1571–1639)
|
Henry (1601–1656)
|
William (c1626–1701)
|
Henry (1664–1727)
|
Sam I (1720–1796)

With Henry we move from shadowy figures, only recorded in legal documents, to real flesh-and-blood characters whose activities and personalities begin to emerge. And with Henry the scene shifts from Gravenhurst to Cardington, and from peasant farmer to minor gentry.

But before opening the Cardington chapter it is worth remembering that there were other Whitbreads, not of Gravenhurst. For example, there were the maltster and the martyr.

The maltster was Henry Whitbread of Hitchin. We know little about him apart from the fact that his son, also Henry, was possibly the first Whitbread brewer. The minute book of the Worshipful Company of Brewers records that in 1622 young Henry was bound apprentice to Thomas Emmerson, Citizen and Brewer of London, for a term of seven years from 5 February.[3]

The martyr was Thomas Harcourt, a Jesuit 'whose real name was Whitbread' and whose arms bear the hind's head as if to prove it. Born in Essex in 1618, he rose to be Superior of his district and later became Provincial of his order. While he was visiting the Belgian colleges of the English Province in 1678, Titus Oates, who had already been expelled from two of the society's colleges, asked to be admitted to membership of the order. On being refused, he threatened that he would be 'either a Jesuit or a Judas'. Later, Harcourt was arrested and after eight months in Newgate gaol he was tried at the Old Bailey and convicted of complicity in the 'Popish Plot', partly on Oates's perjured evidence. He was executed on 20 June 1679.[4]

But, returning to the main Whitbread line, Henry was born in April 1601 at Gravenhurst. His father, William (described as a yeoman on the burial certificate of his wife Elizabeth), had seven children, one of whom died at birth. William had settled the Ion estate on his son Henry shortly before his death in February 1639 and, before the year was out,

Henry had sold Ion to William Alleyn.[5]

In June of that year Henry took a 500-year lease on a property in Cardington from Sir Thomas Savage for £830. This property had formerly been occupied by another Henry Whitbread, and later the same year Sir Thomas sold the property outright for the sum of £2,200. At the same time, Henry took an eighty-year lease on another farm, and two years later, Savage included in his will the Little Farm at Cardington (also occupied by the Cardington Henry). By 1648 Henry's interest in Cardington amounted to some 200 acres, and the following year he leased Great Farm, Cardington, for £230 per annum.[6]

But this came later, after the Civil War. Charles I's attempts to levy ship money on the inland counties of England started surprisingly well, but by 1638 Bedfordshire was paying less than almost anywhere in the country. Indeed, Henry Whitbread appeared in the list of arrears for Nether Gravenhurst in the sum of 7s 9d. In 1639 little or nothing was paid.[7]

However, as early as the 1620s there had been signs of resistance in Bedfordshire to the militia laws, which compelled all able-bodied men to serve in times of national danger or civil unrest. In 1625 the county was badly hit by the plague and even the Trained Bands, troops fully trained and armed, were not mustered in that year. The joint Lieutenants of the county, Henry Earl of Kent and Thomas Earl of Cleveland, complained that the smallness of the county meant that the cost of instruction for the Trained Bands was becoming prohibitive, and the growing dispute between the counties and the Crown over the cost of the militia became a major issue of the Civil War.

The inevitable clash between King and Parliament came in 1640. In Bedfordshire, two Members of Parliament and the Earl of Cleveland (the county's Lieutenant) were loyal to the King. The remaining seven

MPs were active parliamentarians, among them Sir Samuel Luke and his father Sir Oliver, neighbours of Henry Whitbread at Cople, the neighbouring village to Cardington. Support for the King came mainly from the West Country, while Eastern England was mainly for Parliament.[8]

In 1643 the royalists were driven out of Newport Pagnell, which became a garrison town for the parliamentarians under Sir Samuel Luke. The town withstood a siege for nearly two years – quite an achievement in view of the shortage of troops and supplies.

Henry Whitbread was one of nine Captains serving in the garrison.[9] He was appointed muster-master, being responsible for raising money and mustering troops throughout the county. John Bunyan was among those mustered. As with the ship money, Bedfordshire was backward in coming forward with its share of the money required, and surviving contemporary letters written by Sir Samuel Luke show that Henry was constantly being urged to produce money for the troops. In February 1645 the Earl of Manchester's regiment arrived at Newport Pagnell to strengthen the garrison. To make room for them, Luke packed his Colonel and three Captains (including Henry) into his own quarters. 'How their common soldiers will do for beds, I know not,' he wrote. 'All mine…lie three and three in a bed…' Later that year he was demanding coats and breeches for a hundred men. Two in his company 'had but one pair of breeches between them, so that when one was up the other must upon necessity be in his bed'. The soldiers were nine or ten months behind with their pay and 'both soldiers and workmen are very hungry after money'.[10] Part of the problem for Henry was a Captain Pinckney, who had been appointed by Luke to collect funds for the garrison from the counties of East Anglia; he was accused of not handing on some £4,000 destined for the garrison and proved to be, in Luke's words, 'the archest knave that ever man had to deal with'.[11]

In a letter from Sir Samuel Luke to Henry in 1645, he wrote, 'your brother may come when he pleases, and his health will give him leave'. This probably refers to William (born c.1626), as, following the Restoration of the monarchy, King Charles II issued a pardon to 'William Whitbread of Cardington...Gentleman'.[12]

The siege of Newport Pagnell meant that large numbers of Eastern Association forces were quartered in and around Bedford. Among them were Independents, mainly individual enthusiasts opposed to a Presbyterian system of government. Cromwell's army, drawn largely from the eastern counties, united these individuals to become Congregationalists.

In 1650, twelve of these independents, 'all ancient and grave Christians, well known one to another', formed their own group or 'meeting' in Bedford. Three years later they took over the ancient church and hospital of St John's and appointed one of their number, John Gifford (or Giffard), as rector. Gifford had been a Royalist major but had now seen the error of his ways. Later in 1653 William Whitbread of Cardington and his wife Lettice joined Gifford's Independent Congregation, along with John Bunyan, the former tinker from Elstow.[13]

Henry's son William was born in about 1626, possibly at Loughton in Buckinghamshire (where no seventeenth-century parish registers survive), his mother's home. In 1649 he married Lettice Leeds from Croxton in Cambridgeshire. He was appointed a magistrate and Receiver-General for taxes in Bedfordshire; the earliest example of a Bedfordshire Whitbread using heraldic arms appears on William's seal as a magistrate in 1652.[14]

By 1659 William was being included in deputations from Gifford's church to discuss with other churches such matters as replacing a deceased minister and to visit church members in other parishes.[15] However, by 1670 his commitment to the Church seems to have weakened and in January 1670 it was agreed that he should be 'admonished' for 'withdrawing from the Church and the Ordinances of God'. William's reply hinted at his unhappiness with some of the Church's practises but at the same time he desired the freedom 'to associate with you at Church meetings and...join with and assist you therein'.[16]

The congregation were not satisfied with this reply and lack of repentance and sent two of their number to see him. They too found William not 'touched with remorse for his sins...' but apparently surprised that the Church did not see his reply 'as an answer to the admonition'.

A further, stronger letter was sent to William accusing him of 'forsaking the assemblies of the congregation, your casting off the care of the Church in general, and of its members in particular, also your neglect of the Lord's table, and of fasting and prayer with the Church, and that for so long a time as above the space of seven years'. So this was not just a sudden fall from grace but had been building up since 1663 or earlier.

In his reply, William insisted that he should not be forced into confessing anything before his plea had been heard: '...for in no cases are men's pleas allowed after their confessions (which is the surest way of conviction) and yet that only method is limited by yours'. As for forsaking fasting and prayer, he had not been notified of the appointed days for these.[17]

By May 1671 the Church were beginning to lose patience with their unsatisfactory brother and they agreed that he should be told 'that unless the Church speedily discern in him repentance unfeigned, they intend to proceed against him for his miscarriages, by inflicting the censure that God's word judgeth him worthy of'. William failed to attend the next meeting but appears to have given a plausible excuse, 'but give me notice of the next meeting whither, if God spare life, I shall gladly come. Let not any censures pass upon me; you have the unfeigned truth'.[18]

In the meantime William appears to have changed his tune, as, at the next meeting, 'our beloved brother Whitbread was received again into close communion with the Church, he making gracious acknowledgement of his sorrow and repentance for all those miscarriages of which he had been admonished before. In his giving up of himself to the Church again, he did also in the most full manner, without any reservation, commit himself, as also his gifts, in the Lord, to the dispose of the congregation: and did with freeness acknowledge the eldership that is among us, and commit himself to their care and government'.[19]

Whatever was the cause of this sudden rapprochement? We can only guess. Would it be cynical to suggest that the key lies in the words '...as also his gifts...'?

Little else is known about William's life at Cardington. He and Lettice had twelve children, three of whom died in infancy. In 1672 their eldest daughter Martha married John Howard, 'citizen and upholder' of St Sepulchre, London, whose grandson was the famous prison reformer of the same name.[20]

Finally, 1685 saw the first stirrings of political activity in the Whitbread family. William is recorded as voting for William Boteler of Harrold – a Tory and Lord Edward Russell. He might have been expected to support the other Whig candidate, Sir Humphrey Monoux, but his friendship for Boteler persuaded him to act in a way which might have been taken as support for the party that maintained the Test Act to discourage Nonconformists such as himself.[21]

Just as Captain Henry (William's father) took the major step of moving from Gravenhurst to Cardington, so his grandson – also Henry – laid the foundation of the London connection which was to prove so significant to the future fortunes of the family.

William's father was probably the first Whitbread to set foot in London. Until the 1640s, when Henry went to London on behalf of the Newport Pagnell garrison during the Civil War, the Whitbreads had had their feet firmly and permanently on Bedfordshire soil. And yet, only a hundred years later, his three surviving great-grandsons, John, Ive and Samuel, had all set up businesses in London and two of his great-granddaughters had married men whose businesses were based there.

William's son – another Henry – although in fact the third son of William and Lettice, was from his birth in 1664 the male heir. The family lived at the Great Farm (now Maltings Farm) in Cardington and in 1691 Henry married Sarah Ive, not a Bedfordshire girl but the seventeen-year-old daughter of a London merchant, John Ive.

In 1688, following the Glorious Revolution, Land Tax was introduced, replacing archaic taxes dating from pre-Norman days such as tallage, scutage and hidage.[22] Each county was given a quota and a Receiver-General was appointed by the Treasury, responsible for collecting the quarterly payments of tax from the parish collectors. William was Receiver-General in 1693 and was succeeded in 1695 by Henry, who held the appointment until his death in 1727. The post was a responsible one; the parish collectors were not required to travel more than twelve miles and the Receiver had to organise considerable circuits around the county and notify the collectors of his visits to local inns, from where the money was sent by wagons under armed guard to the Receiver's house for onward remittance to the Treasury. The Receiver also had to exercise considerable tact. Not only was he expected to use his influence and authority to galvanise slack collectors into action; he also had to face up to his fellow-landowners, some of whom objected to the way in which the quotas were fixed, the Home Counties bearing a heavier burden than those further from London. Bedfordshire landowners were expected to pay up to 20 per cent of the rents they received, while the more distant counties sometimes paid little more than 5 per cent.

The appointment of William and Henry as Receivers-General of Taxes for Bedfordshire is a measure of just how far up the social scale the family had moved since settling in Cardington in 1649.

Henry, with his wife Sarah, continued his father's respectable and pious lifestyle. As Nonconformists the Whitbreads supported the Whigs, who feared the Catholic James II and prayed for a Protestant succession. In this they were like many of their neighbours; Bedfordshire was described as 'the least addicted to Jacobitism of all England'. However, King James tried to get support for his Declaration of Indulgence, suspending the laws against both Papists and Nonconformists. At the same time he purged the lieutenancy and magistracy of a number of Anglican Tories who wished to maintain the privileges enjoyed by the Church of England, replacing them with Nonconformists; among those who became magistrates for the first time was William Whitbread of Cardington.[23]

Henry and Sarah's prayers were answered in 1688 with the Glorious Revolution and the accession of William III to the throne. They wanted the right to worship as they pleased, rather than under pressure from the Anglican Church. Following William Whitbread's death in 1701, both Henry and Sarah became full members of the Bunyan Meeting.[24]

Sarah died in 1710 at the age of thirty-six leaving five children, including

John, a silkthrower of Whitechapel; Ive, a merchant taylor of Dowgate Hill; and Rachel, who married a London brewer, Oliver Edwards.[25] Seven years later Henry remarried – a wealthy widow, Elizabeth Winch, of St John's, Bedford. She was the daughter of a doctor, Philip Read of Salisbury, from whom she inherited money and land, including a small estate at Little Sodbury in Gloucestershire which would in time be sold to finance her son Samuel's indenture as an apprentice brewer in London.[26]

Henry died in 1727, having fathered a further three sons and a daughter by Elizabeth who returned to Bedford and lived there until her own death in 1746.[27]

Samuel Whitbread I (1720–1796) by Sir Joshua Reynolds PRA, 1786
By kind permission of the Trustees of the Southill Chattels Trust

SAMUEL WHITBREAD I

(1720–96)

*W*e have seen how the Whitbreads moved up the social scale after moving to Cardington in 1639. But with the first Samuel Whitbread the family made further significant progress in three vital areas: firstly, and most obviously, the foundation of the great brewing business – one of the most conspicuous success stories of the Industrial Revolution of the eighteenth century; secondly, the acquisition of more than 10,000 acres of land in Bedfordshire to form what became the Southill estate; and finally, the start of a political tradition resulting in six Whitbreads sitting in the House of Commons for a total of 128 years between 1768 and 1910.[1]

Samuel Whitbread was born at the Great Farm, Cardington on 30 August 1720. It is believed that he was baptised at the Bunyan Meeting in Bedford, as both his parents were members of the Meeting and there is no record of his baptism in Cardington church. When he was only seven years old his father died and the farm passed to Henry's son John, who leased the house with its malting and dovehouse to Thomas Bisgrave of Cardington. Young Samuel and his mother moved to Biddenham and later to Bedford, from where, at the age of twelve, he was sent, together with his elder brother Henry, to be educated by the Reverend Anthony

Munton, vicar of Wollaston, a parish in Northamptonshire some twenty miles from Bedford. This, as he wrote later, 'was all the School learning that I had'.[2] Why his mother should have chosen for her young son an apprenticeship as a brewer – and in London – is unclear, although one of the leading lights in the Bunyan Meeting, Thomas Woodward, was a brewer in Bedford, while Sam's half-sister Rachel's husband, Oliver Edwards, had a brewery in Clerkenwell and his half-brother Ive was well established in London as a hardwareman and jeweller. Whatever the reason, just before his sixteenth birthday Sam became apprenticed to the Master of the Worshipful Company of Brewers, John Wightman of Gilport Street, Clerkenwell.[3] The fee of £300 was very high, but perhaps, as Master Brewer, Wightman would accept no less. Such an apprenticeship normally lasted for seven years, but in December 1742, with seven months still to serve, Samuel set up in business at the Goat brewhouse on the corner of Old Street and Whitecross Street, with two partners, Godfrey and Thomas Shewell.[4]

In the London of the eighteenth century there were four main beers – strong, small, amber and pale. Strong beer (also known as entire or porter) was brewed from brown malt only. Small beer was weaker – the equivalent of mild ale – while the amber and pale ales met a limited demand and were known as "table beers". A small brewhouse on the corner of Old Street and Brick Lane was set aside for the brewing of these table beers, while the Goat brewhouse was kept for the popular porter and small beers.

The brewing process has changed little over the centuries and the quality of the raw materials has always been the basis of a good beer. Samuel Whitbread bought his malt mainly in Bedfordshire and Hertfordshire, and his hops in Kent. Some brewers used dark sugars to cover up the blending of cheaper pale malts in the brewing of porter, but this practice was never allowed in Whitbread's brewhouse.

By 1749 Godfrey Shewell had left the partnership and Whitbread's beer had achieved a reputation as far afield as Ireland, Gibraltar, Jamaica and New York. The same year negotiations began for the purchase of the King's Head brewhouse in Chiswell Street, a move which was to lead to the creation of the greatest of the brewing fortunes of the eighteenth century. Two reasons have been given for this success. First, the tremendous popularity of porter, on which Whitbread concentrated in his new brewery; and secondly, the realisation that porter, which needed maturing for up to a year, was particularly suitable for large-scale brewing. Over the next forty years Whitbread's Chiswell Street brewery was to become one of the spectacles of London. From the 18,000 barrels brewed in the first year at Chiswell Street, production rose to 63,000 barrels in 1760, 150,000 in 1787, and in the year of Samuel's death in 1796 he became the first brewer to produce 200,000 barrels in a year.

But this success was not easily won. Whitbread's daughter Harriot has left a picture of her father sitting up 'four nights a week by his brewhouse copper', only retiring to his room 'when the state of the boiling permitted his quitting... When the rest of the world were asleep, he entered on the worldly business of the day'.[5]

Every penny of profit was needed to pay for the new brewery and for the expansion and improvements which took place over the next forty years. Between 1750 and 1786 over £42,000 was spent on repairs and rebuilding. In addition, Samuel had to find over £70,000 to buy out Thomas Shewell's interest in the business when the latter retired from the partnership in 1761.

Whitbread was quick to recognise the potential offered by steam power for grinding the malt and pumping the liquor (water) from the deep wells beneath the brewery. The first steam engine to be installed in a brewery was at Goodwyn's Red Lion brewhouse at St Katherine's in 1784. Whitbread went to see it and immediately placed an order from the manufacturers Boulton & Watt. The engine was installed at Chiswell Street early in 1785 and was described by Joseph Delafield, one of Whitbread's assistants, as 'the best piece of mechanism I think I ever saw'. With a massive 'Horse Wheel' over twenty feet in diameter, the steam engine, which cost £1,000 to install, saved the costs of twenty-four horses (£960 a year). Together with the Great Storehouse (later known as the Porter Tun Room), with its unsupported timber roof span of sixty-five feet and a capacity of 5,700 barrels, Whitbread's brewery became, in the words of Delafield, 'the wonder of everybody, by which means our pride is become very troublesome, being almost daily resorted to by visitors'.[6] The most famous of these, King George III and Queen Charlotte, came on 24 May 1787, spending more than four hours inspecting the fermenting vessels, cooperage, stables and, of course, the great steam engine. One of the satirical poets of the day, writing under the pseudonym of 'Peter Pindar', produced his 'Instructions to a Celebrated Laureate alias Mr Whitbread's Brewery', lampooning the brewer and the royal visit. In it he has the King offering Sam Whitbread a knighthood, the latter declining, saying, 'He was afraid he was too old'.[7]

Samuel Whitbread was, in the words of a later obituary of his son, 'a man of plain manners and practical good sense... On balancing his books every year, he made all those around him in some measure partners in his business and consequently interested them in his prosperity. It was his practice to distribute this annual donation, in the exact rates of their ranks and services; and beginning with a liberal gift of £500 to a confidential clerk, he was accustomed to extend his bounty to the very horse feeders, to whom he usually gave £5 a piece.'[8]

As a mark of respect and affection for those who had helped him make his fortune, in the 1780s he had portraits of his clerks, Robert Sangster, Joseph Delafield, Jacob Yallowley, Broughton Massey (or Maysey), Samuel Green, David Jennings, J. Phillips and William Slater, painted by artists such as Romney, Gainsborough and Gainsborough's nephew, Dupont. These portraits originally hung either at Bedwell Park, his Hertfordshire home, or at his London house in Portman Square. After his death, and once Southill had been completed by his son, they were reframed and hung in the Library and Dining Room with their names proudly displayed.[9]

Towards the end of his life Whitbread lived comfortably at Bedwell Park, leaving the day-to-day running of the brewery to these clerks or assistants. As he remarked, 'I have been myself always at the head of it, and though not resident, yet frequently there to be consulted and advis'd with and always in my thoughts'.[10]

However successful Whitbread was in business, in his private life he was singularly unlucky. In spite of marrying twice, his life as a married man lasted only seven years. At the age of thirty-eight he married Harriot Hayton or Haydon of Ivinghoe, who bore him two daughters and a son before dying in 1764. (In her memory Samuel founded a charity school for girls in London, with a quaint stipulation that green and white straw hats from Dunstable should be bought for them annually.) Five years later he married Lady Mary Cornwallis, niece of the Archbishop of Canterbury and sister of the celebrated general and Governor of Bengal. She died after a year of marriage, giving birth to a daughter.[11]

By the time Whitbread's only son, also Samuel, came of age in 1785 it was clear that he would be first a politician and only secondly a brewer. Sam senior therefore began to take steps to sell the business he had so proudly built up. In a series of letters to his son he tells his own success story, how the business was raised 'from a very small beginning and by great assiduity in a very long course of years, even fifty years, and with the highest credit in every view by honest and fair dealing…and the beer universally approved, and the quantity brewed annually great indeed amounted…to 180 thousand barrels and at commencement was only 18 thousand… There never was the like before, nor probably ever will be again, in the Brewing Trade.' He goes on gently to chide his son: 'You have no inducement to continue the Trade…therefore…don't think of continuing of it but sell it.' Later he seems to have changed his tactics. 'And so very clear I am that you should not have any thought of continuing the Trade, I intend to dispose of it myself…' The prospective purchasers were the Harvey family of Norwich; the asking price, £300,000.[12] Fortunately for Samuel Whitbread's successors, negotiations were still in progress when he died in 1796.

As we have seen, profits from the brewery were ploughed back into the business. Any surplus was wisely invested, mainly in land. As Sam Whitbread wrote to his daughter Harriot Gordon, 'English land is the only security and best to live on the income of it, if proprietors will submit to the interest it brings, which scarce anyone will do.'[13] As early as 1760 he bought the lease of Fenlake Barns for £3,800, borrowing £2,200 from his half-brother Ive as he could not afford to take money out of the business. Over the next ten years he bought a further 430 acres, including Bedwell Park in Hertfordshire for £8,000. The year 1771 saw the purchase of Ive Whitbread's 530-acre Cardington estate because 'it was the place of my birth and inheritance of my Father's… the Parish where our family had lived 150 years'.[14]

In 1777 Samuel Whitbread made a very shrewd investment in several hundred acres in West Thurrock, Essex, which included farmland, the hamlet of Purfleet and an ancient chalk quarry. The original reason for buying the land was that it would provide hay for the 160-odd dray horses at the brewery; the hay could be easily transported up the Thames and unloaded at a wharf convenient to Chiswell Street. A substantial twenty-six-room house was built in 1790, and the lease on the quarry was bought from the Bricklayers' Company of London in 1794. The quarry produced quantities of lime, much in demand for the building boom in London at that time. John Clarkson, who with his brother Thomas had known Whitbread through their active involvement in the anti-slavery movement, was appointed to run Purfleet. He built it into a flourishing business which, after it had passed to the second Samuel Whitbread, produced receipts of over £5,000 a year.[15]

By 1785 Whitbread senior had acquired over 4,500 acres in eight counties at a cost of over £100,000, and with his son's coming of age had become resigned to the latter's indifference to 'the Trade'. He therefore determined to give young Sam an alternative source of income as well as a strong country base for the political career which appeared to be his destiny.[16] Between 1786 and 1795 his purchases of land increased four-fold, including 1,100 acres in Old Warden and 1,500 in Elstow. At Southill the 4th Viscount Torrington had built a large house in the 1720s. His extravagancies came to a head in 1777 when Capability Brown was engaged to enlarge the park. Soon the Viscount's debts exceeded £90,000 and his friend the Duke of Portland became a trustee of the estate in an attempt to rescue him. The house was rented, fully furnished, for £100 a year by Lord Polwarth, who wrote in 1779 that Southill was 'a place built and fitted up by an Ideot, with great expence in which every room and every office is good in itself, but every room and every office stands in the wrong place.' By 1781 Polwarth was dead and Torrington's problems returned. In 1794 Samuel Whitbread loaned him £7,500 and the following year Whitbread paid off the mortgages, bought out the annuitants and purchased the estate for £95,000.[17]

Thus, when old Sam Whitbread died in 1796, his son inherited an estate of 12,300 acres, of which 80 per cent was in Bedfordshire, with annual rents totalling nearly £22,000 – about £700,000 at today's values.

It is a measure of Sam Whitbread's energy and industry that, in addition to founding and developing his great brewing business and amassing a country estate second in Bedfordshire only to that of the Duke of Bedford himself, he should have found time to sit in Parliament for twenty-eight years and to begin a family parliamentary tradition that was to last for 142 years.

In 1767, at the age of forty-seven, he showed interest in contesting one of the two parliamentary seats for the county of Bedford which had become vacant through the tragic death (from a riding accident) of the Marquess of Tavistock. The following year he was elected for the Borough along with Richard Vernon, the Duke's candidate (and brother-in-law).[18]

Although an infrequent speaker in the House of Commons, the causes he espoused were more those of a radical Whig than of a Tory. For the first five years of his parliamentary career he campaigned against corruption in the Government and particularly in the electoral system. He was an independent Tory, for example voting with the Whigs to expel Wilkes, but with the Government on the Middlesex Election in 1773. In 1780 the Government whip John Robinson noted: 'Mr Whitbread is a very doubtful, uncertain man for either side, but if either way I think may be reckoned more hopeful to go in general with Government.'

The year 1781 saw growing opposition to the Government of Lord North and its prosecution of the war in America. General Cornwallis (Sam Whitbread's brother-in-law) surrendered to the American insurgents at Yorktown and the following year a motion was carried in the House of Commons opposing the continuation of the American war. Lord North had wanted to resign for some time but King George III would not let him go. Sam Whitbread was one of the four 'rats' – Tories who were ambivalent in their support of the Government and who eventually forced North's resignation.[19]

He was also one of the first to draw attention to the slave trade. By the mid-eighteenth century, British maritime supremacy had put much of the slave trade into British hands, mainly operating from Bristol and the West Country ports. According to Samuel Whitbread's daughter Harriot Gordon, 'he was really the first man who mentioned the Slave Trade in the House of Commons and called Mr Pitt's attention to it, finding Sir William Dolben, member for the University of Oxford, eager to take a share in the Conversation, rather than Debate, he most gladly resigned the cause in the House into what he said were better and abler hands. But the early and small meetings to enquire into the Slave Trade were held in his drawing-room in Portman Square.'[20]

In 1790 Sam Whitbread was reluctantly persuaded to step down as MP for Bedford to allow his twenty-six-year-old son to enter Parliament (as a Whig).[21] Thereafter the old man was returned for Steyning, a 'Rotten Borough' in Sussex, (the Duke of Norfolk's candidate having been unseated for bribery), until his death in 1796. His daughter believed that 'under his growing infirmities' (he had had periods of illness in 1781 and 1789) he only returned to Parliament because of the revival of the slave trade issue. '…this I believe he never would have been…but for some mental promise he had made to himself never to desert that cause, and in that only he had the satisfaction of seeing his son always vote with him. Their policies in other respects had widely differed, but each had too powerful a mind to act by another's judgment.'[22]

The younger Samuel Whitbread was to see the slave trade finally abolished in England in 1806.

Father Sam's fellow MPs were not sure what to make of him. Years later, when two of his son's contemporaries were discussing him, he was referred to as 'an exceedingly odd man'. True, he did not conform to the usual image of the aristocratic Tory, being semi-educated, but with 'a mind endowed with great resources'; devout, but totally unashamed of being so; enormously rich, but with a new and impressive wealth honestly obtained. In the eighteenth century most wealth came either from lucrative Government jobs or from profitable sidelines in the Far East or the West Indies. Whitbread (despite Walpole's allusion to his 'insolent wealth') brought a new respectability to riches. Princess Amelia, daughter of George III, summed it up thus: 'I would not give a straw to be a peer in this country – no, give me a good brewhouse; that is what makes one considerable here'.

On his seventieth birthday, in 1790, Samuel Whitbread sat down to write his 'Reflections' in the form of a long prayer addressed to his Maker. This included the words: 'O may I never forget my God, beware of covetousness, and be mindful of the wants of others, and never turn my face from any poor man that the face of God may never be turned away from me, and, while I have yet time, do good.'[23]

He was indeed famed for his philanthropy. In Bedfordshire he paid for the education of Cardington children; in the early 1790s he arranged with his friend Matthew Boulton, the Birmingham steam engine manufacturer, 'for half a dozen healthy boys, 13 to 16 years, with open countenances' to be sent from Cardington to Birmingham (on foot, incidentally!) to ease his labour situation and to relieve the poor parents of Cardington burdened with over-large families. With his neighbour and cousin John Howard he improved many of the houses in

Cardington. The diarist John Byng (later Viscount Torrington) wrote that they 'strive which shall most benefit and adorn it; for what cannot the riches of the one and the charity of the other accomplish?'[24]

When Howard was Sheriff of Bedfordshire in 1773 his responsibilities in respect of Bedford gaol led him to examine the conduct of neighbouring county gaols and he visited Northampton, Leicester, Huntingdon and Cambridge. Among other things he was shocked to find that prisoners on remand (i.e. awaiting trial) were forced to pay the gaoler for their board and lodging, and he was prompted to investigate all the Country's gaols; it was Whitbread who suggested that the findings of this tour should be compiled into a book. Furthermore, two of his brewhouse clerks, Delafield and Catherwood, arranged Howard's documents in some sort of order, for, in the words of Sam's daughter Harriot, '[Howard] himself had no natural or acquired Idea at all of arranging them, for he never was in a habit of anything that required methodical arrangement'. When the book was finished it was Whitbread who showed it to the Speaker who in turn passed it to the judges 'who very much commended and approved the same'.[25]

Somewhat surprisingly the two friends fell out over the result of the 1774 election. Whitbread and Howard both stood as Tory candidates for the two Bedford seats. They were defeated but, as was often the case in the days before universal suffrage, they both petitioned against the result on the grounds of the ineligibility of some of the voters. The committee hearing the petition decided that Whitbread and one of the two Whigs, Mr Wake, should be declared elected.[26] From then on the relationship between the two seems to have been soured, in spite of Whitbread paying all the election expenses as well as offering to employ an artist to illustrate Howard's *State of the Prisons*. When this was finally published in 1777, Whitbread was disappointed to find that instead of the dedication which Howard had mentioned 'when he wanted my assistance…he never so much as mentioned my name'.[27]

One morning at breakfast at Bedwell, Sam Whitbread's butler brought him a petition from a beggar who was dumb from cancer of the tongue and claimed to have been turned out of a London hospital as being incurable. Whitbread could not believe that such a thing was possible, but having checked next day at St Bartholomew's Hospital (close by the Chiswell Street brewhouse) he found that incurables were indeed discharged to make room for others. Six months later he settled £4,000 on the Middlesex Hospital to fund a cancer ward which still bears his name today.[28]

Samuel Whitbread died on 11 June 1796 at Bedwell, 'as was his wish...with all his children in the house, his son by his bedside, with the windows open, and the sashes thrown up, in his 76th year, having been paralytic of one side above three years, and having had at times apoplexy in one of which seizures he died – having first blest God for seeing the light of another day'.[29]

The generosity for which he was so conspicuous continued after his death – his will covered 126 pages – and a writer remarked that his 'abilities, integrity, benevolence and public spirit will transmit his character to the latest posterity'.[30] His simple faith continued to the end, as did his concern for his children. Five years before his death he wrote: 'I pray for opportunity to take leave of my dear children and recommend them to the mercy and favour of God and advise them against waste of time especially in bed as incompatible with duty to God and man…and grant O my God that I may at last make a decent and happy exit in thy own due time and after this painful and miserable life ended enjoy a glorious eternity through the merits of our dear redeemer Jesus Christ.'[31]

Samuel Whitbread II (1764–1815) by Thomas Gainsborough RA, 1788
By kind permission of the Trustees of the Southill Chattels Trust

SAMUEL WHITBREAD II

(1764–1815)

'*Who is the greatest Englishman of our time?*'
To this question, asked in 1815, the poet Byron replied: 'Beau Brummel'; the Prince Regent 'Wellington'; while the verdict of the editor of *The Times* was, perhaps surprisingly, 'Samuel Whitbread'.[1]

True, this answer was given in the aftermath of Sam Whitbread's tragic death at the age of fifty-one. But it was, as we shall see, but one of the many fulsome tributes paid to this radical Whig politician.

Samuel Whitbread II was born in 1764. His mother died six weeks later and the young Sam was brought up by his grandmother. He went to Eton with a private tutor and soon made friends with young Charles Grey and William Lambton. From there he proceeded first to Christ Church, Oxford, and the following year to St John's, Cambridge – why his father removed him from Oxford is not clear. At Cambridge he was reunited with Grey and Lambton, and first made the acquaintance of someone who was to become a more or less permanent member of his family circle, Thomas Adkin. The son of a Norfolk curate, Adkin was witty and extravagant and did not find favour with old Sam Whitbread. 'He is a man of loose character, not fit for your acquaintance,' Sam wrote to his son.[2]

27

On leaving Cambridge at the age of twenty the young Whitbread was sent abroad, not on the fashionable Grand Tour of France and Italy, but to Hamburg, Stockholm, St Petersburg, Warsaw, Berlin and Munich before heading south through Switzerland to Florence for a brief visit. His companion on this trip, no doubt carefully chosen by his father, was William Coxe, future archdeacon and writer. Dr Johnson endorsed the choice of Coxe: 'For the purpose there was not, he thought, any other so proper or so equal in the kingdom.'[3]

While he was abroad young Sam received a letter from his father about his future in the brewery. 'You express yourself handsomely and feelingly on the subject of trade. But pray don't make a burden of it to hurt your spirits, for it is a matter that you and myself can part with. And you would have two good reasons to give; one that it would take too much of your time from other employment in life that you are from education more inclined to yourself. The second is that you have as much affluence as can make a reasonable man happy.'[4] What was the 'other employment' the father had in mind? Had the political flame already been kindled in young Sam's mind?

Returning from abroad in the autumn of 1785, Sam Whitbread settled down to the business of brewing in Chiswell Street. It was a busy time for Whitbread and son. Steam power had been introduced into the brewery that year, a ten horse-power Boulton & Watt engine installed by the great John Rennie, builder of Waterloo, London and Southwark bridges.[5] But Sam's heart was not really in 'the Trade'. His friendship at Eton and Cambridge with Charles Grey drew him into the Devonshire House Set, headed by the beautiful Georgiana, Duchess of Devonshire; Sam came into contact with her many admirers, among them Charles James Fox, Sheridan and the Prince of Wales, and the renewed friendship with Grey brought another ingredient into the life of the young Whitbread. In the summer of 1786 he fell in love with Grey's sister Elizabeth. This displeased old Sam Whitbread, and the relationship between father and son, never more than cordial, can seldom have been at a lower level. At the age of twenty-two young Sam was packed off to Europe once again, in spite of his protests. Among his many letters to his 'beloved Bess' was this riddle, the answer to each question being the word Grey:

> What is seen in the morning proclaims a fine day;
> What widows put on when their grief fades away.
> Is the name of a girl who shall be my own;
> Is the name of a girl who was hurled from the throne.
> Is the name of all names in which I delight
> But a name I <u>will</u> change in the Devil's own spite. [6]

They were married in January 1788 at Falloden, the Grey family home in Northumberland, and moved to Woolmers Park in Hertfordshire, close to his father's home at Bedwell.

In the general election of 1790, Charles Grey was adopted as Whig candidate for Northumberland and it was suggested that Sam Whitbread should stand for Bedford. This meant that either there would be the unprecedented situation of Whig son standing against Tory father, or the elder Sam Whitbread (by now seventy years of age) would have to step down. A deputation from the Borough of Bedford found the son visiting his father at Cardington. When the proposal was put to them, old Sam 'strongly objected'. A two-hour discussion in the garden shook the old man's resolve and his consent was slowly and reluctantly given – only to be withdrawn a few minutes afterwards. But by then young Sam had left the house with the deputation, and the father, unable to open the garden door (it had 'a spring latch which the old man had forgotten'), failed to reach Bedford before his son addressed the electors, thereby virtually securing his election to Parliament. Whether or not young Sam's handling of his father was in any way underhand, it certainly rankled with the old man, who wrote a few days later, 'I am pretty well, but not recovered the storm to my soul, and my son is not kind nor respectful.'[7]

Whitbread entered the House in November 1790 and within days was on his feet attacking the Government for wasting money on military preparations. He soon attracted the attention of the Whig leadership and was entrusted with moving several motions criticising Government policy. He identified himself with the great social issues of slavery and civil rights, but his most radical reforms were the Wage Regulation Bills of 1795 and 1800.[8]

The 1795 Bill enabled magistrates to fix the minimum wage payable to agricultural labourers. While agreeing with the economic liberals that the price of labour should find its own level without legislative interference, Whitbread held that the increasing misery of the labouring poor demanded that an exception should be made. Labourers should be paid enough to keep themselves, free from a slavish dependency. While the Bill received some support, others feared that if wages were raised to meet prices it would be difficult to lower them when prices fell. The Bill was defeated mainly because Pitt promised a Poor Law of his own which would be more comprehensive.

Whitbread reintroduced the Bill in 1800, only to be defeated again, but by now he was giving his mind to reform of the Poor Law itself and in 1807 he introduced a Bill whose object was to make the Poor Laws obsolete by striking at what he saw as the root cause of poverty itself – ignorance and vice. If the poor were educated, they would be able to cope with their poverty without the need for relief, so he proposed that every child between the ages of seven and fourteen, and who was unable to pay, should receive two years' free education. When this idea was rejected, Sam Whitbread threw his weight (and his money) behind the establishment of schools for poor children, like those set up by Joseph Lancaster, who in 1798 had opened a school in Southwark where a notice read, 'All who will, may send their children and have them educated freely and those who do not wish to have education for nothing, may pay for it if they please.' In order to help the poor to help themselves, Whitbread suggested the establishment of a national bank and national insurance – both ideas well ahead of their time but thought to be just too radical to attract the support of the Tory squires.[9]

A very tall, imposing figure, Sam Whitbread was not a man to disguise his political beliefs and allegiances. At the time of his son William Henry's death, a man recalled Sam attending the Bunyan Meeting in Bedford and arriving after the first hymn and in the middle of 'the long prayer', dressed in a blue coat and a white hat which he hung, complete with blazing orange and blue cockade (the Whig colours), on a nail on a wooden pillar 'conspicuously before the eyes of all the congregation, to the great scandal, we have been often told since, of the serious people. But the offence was soon forgiven. Indeed so popular then was Mr Whitbread, especially among the dissenters, that had he invaded the pulpit, and hung his hat at the back of the minister, he would have been forgiven.'

In 1805 Whitbread achieved national fame over the impeachment of Lord Melville,[10] the last occasion in English history on which this antiquated piece of legal machinery was used. Impeachment was a judicial process whereby ministers and others in public positions were accused by the House of Commons and tried by the Lords for serious crimes and misdemeanours committed in office. Henry Dundas, 1st Viscount Melville, head of a clan of able, avaricious Tory Scots, was Treasurer of the Navy for seventeen years. During this time he allowed his paymaster – another Scot, Alexander Trotter – to take the naval balances and lay them out at interest with Coutts the banker. Trotter pocketed the interest and lent money to Melville. Whitbread moved a series of resolutions attacking Melville's conduct and demonstrating the risks to which the public funds had been exposed. These were carried on the casting vote of the Speaker – perhaps the most dramatic event in all parliamentary history. Two months later the House of Commons decided to impeach Melville, and Whitbread was entrusted with the management of the impeachment.

On the morning of 29 April 1806 Westminster Hall simmered with excitement as the actors in this drama took their places. Step into that great hall today, which once witnessed the trials of William Wallace, Guy Fawkes and Charles I and Edmund Burke's impeachment of Warren Hastings, and imagine the scene for yourself. First, the Speaker and members of the House of Commons proceeded to their seats; then the judges, heralds, lords, barons, viscounts and bishops in procession. Finally the earls, dukes, Archbishops of Canterbury and York, the Lord Chancellor and the royal princes and, last of all, the Prince of Wales himself. Whitbread opened the proceedings with a powerful speech lasting three and a half hours. It was a task which would have tested the skill of an experienced advocate, let alone a forty-two-year-old brewer. Yet it drew from the Lord Chancellor himself the comment: 'Although as you may suppose, I do not mean to convey any idea of the impression made upon me by your speech *as a judge to decide upon the impeachment;* yet I cannot refuse myself the pleasure of expressing the satisfaction I received from the ability and genius displayed in every part of it. Detailed as it was, it appeared to have no details. There was no episode or digression, but everything connected with and embodied in the subject.'

The trial lasted fifteen days and resulted in Melville being acquitted on all charges, although the majorities in some cases were small enough to condemn him in the eyes of the public. He never held office again.

Whitbread was much admired for the thoroughness and zest with which he worked, both during the preparation and the trial itself. He may have attracted some criticism for the style of his oratory but he showed that, in spite of the overwhelming Tory majority in the House of Commons, results could be achieved by the Whigs, especially when the conviction of the rightness of their views was shared by many thousands in the country.

After the death of Pitt in 1806 the Whigs had their first taste of office since Sam Whitbread had entered the House some fifteen years earlier. Lord Grenville was asked to form a Government and, together with Fox, decided to broaden the ministry by including some of Henry Addington's followers. This coalition of the Old (Fox) Whigs and the New (Grenville) Whigs was dubbed the Ministry of All the Talents, and Whitbread, after his success in procuring the impeachment of Melville (the actual trial was yet to come), naturally expected to be included. However, during the formation of the government, Grey – according to Lord Holland – 'somewhat hastily answered for Mr Whitbread's declining both title and office...'[11] When told this, Whitbread drily remarked, 'I might have been left to give the refusal myself.' Whether or not this was a genuine misunderstanding, it led to a temporary breach of friendship between himself and the Whig leadership. He wrote to Grey, 'My constituents received me with looks of surprise, and having stupidly supposed that whenever the turn did happen I should be among the first wanted, conclude from my exclusion that those who know me more intimately and are of course better judges, differ from them very widely in opinion as to my usefulness, or that I have made a bargain about a peerage. In short I feel that I have lost all the reputation my consistency and effort of fifteen years, added to the triumph of the last session, have procured for me.' At the back of his mind was a feeling of inferiority. He sensed that he had been rejected by the Whig aristocracy on account of his background, or 'want of birth' as he put it in a letter to Grey. There was something incongruous about a radical Whig who was also a wealthy brewer and in the same letter he refers to '…trade, which you appeared to think disqualified me for every high situation'.

Fox's death later the same year caused a rekindling of the flame of anger between Whitbread and his brother-in-law, although the electors of Westminster recognised Sam as Fox's spiritual heir, inviting him to succeed the great man as Member for Westminster. But he remained loyal to the Bedford electorate, confidently stating, 'I have been too long before you and the public, and in all the other relations of my life I have acted too immediately under your eye as to have left any part of my character unexplored by you. You have it in your power to bestow upon me the proudest distinction I shall ever covet.'[12]

From the end of 1807, the split between Whitbread and the other leading Whigs seems to have widened, particularly over the issues of war and foreign affairs. Grey tried to heal the split with the offer of a peerage, perhaps well-intentioned but certainly lacking in tact. In a letter to a friend, Whitbread spurned the offer: 'I could not but be indignant at the offer, especially so made; and I was immediately convinced that as an active friend he could have no opinion of me at all, or he would not have dreamt of disabling me and disgracing me…'[13]

The Whig party disintegrated further in 1809, with Whitbread,

Folkestone and Burdett breaking away from Grenville and Grey. As the regular Opposition relaxed, Whitbread and his followers were described as 'the only forcible organs of Liberal principles in the House'. He continually attacked corruption and negligence; among his targets was the Duke of York, whom he criticised for the alleged sale of commissions in the Army through his mistress, Mary Anne Clarke. He forced Lord Chatham's resignation over the disastrous expedition against the Scheldt in 1809, ending his speech with the words: 'the memory of the dead and the honour of the Army call for vengeance upon the authors of this expedition. I trust in God that the House will attend to the call.' The following year he was one of the few who opposed the Regency Bill, appointing the Prince of Wales Regent to act for his father the King during his indisposition.[14]

In 1811 it appeared that the Whigs might again have the chance of office. Despite opposition from the Grenvillites it was arranged that Sam Whitbread should be Home Secretary. However, once again the cup was dashed from his lips; the Prince Regent insisted on maintaining in office the Tory administration of Perceval, and for this the Whigs never forgave him. The somewhat strange championing of Princess Caroline (later Queen) by the Whigs, led by Whitbread, was motivated less by their desire to help her than by their determination to harm the Prince Regent.[15]

The last two years of Sam Whitbread's life were spent advocating a negotiated peace with France. Never a popular attitude, anything that smacked of pacifism at this time brought scorn and veiled accusations of treachery which must have sapped even the strongest spirit. But he was in fact unconsciously prophesying the savageries which Europe has seen twice in the last century with chilling accuracy. 'Contemplate if you can with composure these two mighty empires exerting their utmost efforts each for the destruction of the other, and think upon it if you can without horror that before the contest be ended, one or the other must be destroyed... It is a prospect which I do not think, with the blessing of God, it is necessary even in the present disastrous state of the world to look forward to. If it be, how trifling are the woes and calamities already suffered by mankind to those which are yet to come.'[16]

Scorned as being unpatriotic, Whitbread claimed that he was doing no more than following the humane teaching of Fox. 'I willingly acknowledge myself his true and genuine disciple. Would to God I could feel myself, as I have often done, secure under the impenetrable aegis of his eloquence. I am not the apologist of France. I am the advocate of England.'[17] Interestingly, Napoleon himself, in exile on the island of St Helena, remarked that 'Fox's death was one of the fatalities of my career',[18] meaning that if Fox had lived, he might have secured a negotiated peace with England.

But active as he was, we must not think of Sam Whitbread solely in terms of his parliamentary career. Like other Whitbreads before and since, he was essentially a Bedfordshire man. At the time when his father was completing his purchases of land in Bedfordshire, Sam Whitbread was living at Woolmers Park in Hertfordshire. On the death of his father in 1796 he engaged the fashionable Whig architect, Henry Holland, to modernise and remodel Southill, bought from the Byng family the previous year.[19] Four years later he moved in with his family, although the work was far from complete. It was something of a homecoming for the young politician. Though born at Cardington, he had spent most of his life in Hertfordshire; now he was to live within six miles both of his birthplace and of Shillington – 'the ancient place of the Whitbreads', as his father had described it.

Sam Whitbread built up the estate by buying over 2,000 acres, while at the same time selling outlying holdings in Bedfordshire as well as in other counties. From his father he had inherited about 12,300, acres of which 1,800 lay outside the county. Following the sales and purchases outlined above, by 1815 (the year of his death) the estate totalled about 12,000 acres – almost all in Bedfordshire. He supervised the enclosures of the parishes of Southill, Bedford St Mary, Elstow, Cardington and Wilstead between 1797 and 1809. Under the Enclosure Acts the old system of ownership of scattered plots and strips of land, dating from the days of the medieval open fields, was replaced by individual hedged or fenced fields and farms. The population increase of 43 per cent in England in the second half of the eighteenth century led to calls for a more efficient and productive method of farming. The estate was managed by James and Thomas Lilburne, and between 1797 and 1813 (following the enclosures) the gross rental from it increased by about 48 per cent – rather less than in other areas where increases of 70 to 90 per cent were not uncommon as a result of the enclosures. Sam Whitbread may have seen larger increases as being 'politically incorrect', and incompatible with his position as a local Member of Parliament.[20]

He threw himself wholeheartedly into the life of the county, sitting daily as a magistrate in the Justice Room at Southill,[21] building and improving farms and cottages on the estate, joining with his neighbour the Duke of Bedford in experiments to improve livestock and crops and becoming a leading member of the Bedfordshire Agricultural Society, from which he won several silver trophies which remain at Southill today. He was Colonel of the Volunteer Battalion, submitting willingly to the rigours of days and nights in camp. His father had bequeathed the sum of £8,000 to build an infirmary in Bedford; Sam Whitbread not only built it – he, together with the Duke of Bedford, managed it as well.[22]

But it was not all work. Sam enjoyed to the full the popular country sports, particularly hunting and shooting. His son Samuel Charles described him as 'a perfect horseman and the best judge of a horse I have ever known'.[23] He was instrumental in the formation of the Oakley Hunt, formerly a private pack belonging to the Duke of Bedford, and together with Lee Antonie, the Duke and Lord Tavistock, ran the hunt until 1810, when his health and increasing weight forced him to give up hunting. He wrote wistfully to Lee Antonie, for ten years a fellow Member of Parliament for Bedford, 'I miss the chase exceedingly. The want of it takes the zest off Southill at this time of year.'[23]

The Whitbreads frequently entertained at Southill, despite the fact that Elizabeth had bouts of ill-health. Apart from members of the Whig coterie, John Opie the portrait painter and his wife Amelia were frequent visitors, as were Sawrey Gilpin and the engraver S. W. Reynolds. A young man, William Prinsep, has left an account of his visit to Southill in about 1809.[24] He describes his nervous arrival at the house where he was greeted by Tom Adkin, 'whose business it was to make every stranger feel quite at home at once, shown everything and every place and told where and when to come to the different assemblies during the day'. After dinner (taken much earlier than we are accustomed to today) a four-horse dray would take guests round the estate and Sam would show them 'the plantations he was then engaged at enormous expense in making on the bare sand hills which surrounded him on all sides. People thought him mad upon such a wild venture, but forty years afterwards I was driven round in like manner by the son [William Henry] over the same ground and he was making £1200 per annum by railway sleepers from the mere thinning of these plantations.'

Sam Whitbread's brewing activities confirmed his father's worst fears. He was not really interested in 'the Trade'. Writing to Charles Grey, he described the Brewery as 'a tolerably easy source of income without making too many demands on my time'.[25] Between 1796 and 1800, his financial interest in the firm fell from £250,000 – the entire partnership capital – to £66,000 (less than a fifth), and some of this must have been needed to pay Holland and the many craftsmen who were working at Southill at this time. In fact, Whitbread's surviving account books show that between 1796 and 1803 payments were made to Holland totalling £54,000. To raise this money he took in partners at the Brewery, first, in 1798 his father's clerks Yallowley and Sangster (whose portraits hang at Southill) and Timothy Brown, a rich radical banker. The following year three additional partners were included.[26] These transactions might today be described as a switch of investments – out of industry and into property. But the truth is that Whitbread's heart was elsewhere than in Chiswell Street; it was in the House of Commons, at Southill and, as we shall see, for a period at Drury Lane Theatre.

The playwright Richard Brinsley Sheridan was a long-standing friend of Samuel Whitbread. Sheridan's second wife, Esther, was related to the Greys; Whitbread and Charles Grey were her trustees, a thankless task in view of Sheridan's debts and the inextricable entanglement of her money and his. In 1809 Drury Lane Theatre, managed and part-owned by Sheridan (and built fifteen years before by Henry Holland), was totally destroyed by fire. This was a disaster for Sheridan; the building was under-insured, it was heavily mortgaged, and above all it had given him an easy platform for the revival of his plays. Charitably but unwisely, Whitbread was persuaded to head the committee for rebuilding the theatre. The task was a formidable one. The debts on the old theatre ran to more than £400,000, but Whitbread and his committee raised the necessary funds in two years. The new theatre took less than twelve months to build and opened in October 1812.[27]

It might be thought that such energy and generosity would have been gratefully acknowledged by the wayward playwright. After all, it was by no means the first time that Whitbread had rescued Sheridan; earlier, Sheridan had found himself so deeply in debt to his benefactor that he had invited him to his house to take his choice of his pictures. Gainsborough's *The Painter's Daughters* was the result. But a bitter resentment grew in Sheridan's mind, partly because Whitbread (wisely) would allow him no part in the management of the theatre, and partly because he refused him money to keep his seat in the Commons in 1812 (Sheridan's membership of the House of Commons rendered him immune from arrest for debt). A series of pathetic letters from Sheridan – some touched with bitterness – show the depths of despair reached by the playwright, once the toast of the London stage but now a whining, drunken debtor.[28]

Many of those who took £100 shares in the theatre were friends and neighbours in Bedfordshire; some in fact were employees – the gardener at Southill, Whitbread's agent Wilshere, the butler John Weir. The realisation that the theatre was not successful enough to repay these small investors began to prey on Whitbread's mind. There is some evidence to suggest that he was not physically well; he complained of headaches and wrote to his sister Lady St John, 'I am not ill; but I am not well...' Since 1809 he had been suffering from depression, and with it a sense of being persecuted. 'I am become an object of universal abhorrence.' 'The world will point and scoff at me. The populace will pull down my house.' He was also clearly suffering from overwork. His friends urged him to rest from his parliamentary activities. In March 1815 his wife told a friend that she hoped 'a little country air and comparative idleness will be of much benefit to him'. On 1 July his colleague Brougham, seriously alarmed, told Grey, 'If you see Whitbread or Lady Elizabeth, do for God's sake insist on their immediately going away, not to Southill where he works, but anywhere else, and urge her to keep him <u>absolutely idle</u> for two months at least'.[29]

Five days later, on the morning of 6 July 1815, at his house in Dover Street, Samuel Whitbread locked the door of his dressing-room and, standing in front of a mirror, cut his throat with a razor.[30]

The explanations for this terrible act are many – but are mostly implausible. 'It was the damned theatre,' wrote a close political friend. Lord Ossulston commented, 'How could it ever enter into the scheme of providence that a man like Whitbread, the best man in all the relations of life and the most valuable person, should put an end to his impartial [sic] life because the affairs of Drury Lane was going on ill?' Others believed him to be in debt, but with a sizeable estate and the brewery going well, this seems an unlikely reason for suicide. Some have even connected his death with the news of Napoleon's defeat at Waterloo. The official verdict of the inquest was that 'he died by his own hand – but in a deranged state of mind'. From the medical evidence that has survived it would appear that he was suffering from a form of meningitis. The Drury Lane and Napoleon theories were doubtless put about by his friends and opponents respectively.

The whole country was stunned by the news of Whitbread's death. Tributes poured in from all sides. The editor of *The Times* described him as 'England's greatest and most useful citizen'. Wilberforce declared that 'there had never existed a more complete Englishman.' Even the Prince Regent, the target of many of Whitbread's verbal thrusts, is said to have remarked, 'Whitbread was an honest man.' Sir Samuel Romilly called him 'the promoter of every liberal scheme for improving the condition of mankind, the zealous advocate of the oppressed and the undaunted opposer of every species of corruption and ill-administration'.[31] In modern times, his biographer Roger Fulford has described him in contemporary terms as 'a parliamentary ombudsman – perhaps the earliest example known to English political history'.[32]

But perhaps the last word should be left to Sam Whitbread himself, a declaration which seems to echo the simple conviction of his father: 'I have no object but the public good; I want nothing: I seek nothing. If I do wrong, 'tis because I am not wise enough to do right.'

William Henry Whitbread (1795–1867) by Sir Francis Grant RA
By kind permission of the Trustees of the Southill Chattels Trust

Chapter Four

WILLIAM HENRY *(1795–1867)* and SAMUEL CHARLES WHITBREAD *(1796–1879)*

W illiam Henry Whitbread had neither the business acumen of his grandfather nor the political zeal of his father. In the words of Roger Fulford in his biography of Samuel Whitbread II, William Henry 'lacked the ability and sensibility of the Whitbread family'.[1] And yet, as we shall see, he inherited their sense of duty to their county and their generosity with both their time and their money to those less fortunate than themselves.

William Henry was born on 4 January 1795 at Woolmers Park, his father's home in Hertfordshire. Together with his elder sister Elizabeth and his younger brother Samuel Charles, he was taught by a tutor, Nicholas Salmon, who wrote to their father that they were 'indolent and inattentive. With regard to flogging, I really believe that with them it would not prove a remedy fit to be frequently applied'.[2]

The boys spent much of their time at the stables and with the keepers, 'very much to the disadvantage of their education or their good standing among the local gentry'.[3] Samuel Charles was his mother's favourite; perhaps William was a rebellious child? However, in spite of this inauspicious start, William went to Eton – to the house of the notorious Dr Keate, although he was temporarily removed because of an outbreak of scarlet fever. He entered Trinity College, Cambridge but in 1815 his father, obsessed with the notion that Cambridge was an unhealthy place, moved both his sons to Edinburgh, and it was here that they learned the shocking news of their father's suicide.[4] With this came, far too early for William, the inheritance of the brewery, Southill and the estate, all encumbered with debts accumulated by his father, together with a responsibility towards his widowed mother.

His sister Elizabeth was by now married to Captain the Hon. William Waldegrave, later to become the 8th Earl, and his family did what they could to help Whitbread with his business affairs. While an undergraduate at Trinity William met Judith Pigott, a lady of lowly birth; some said she was one of the Trinity bed-makers or 'bedders', employed by the College to clean, dust and make the beds in the undergraduates' rooms. Whatever her station in life, she and William were married at St Luke's, Chelsea, in 1819; she was twenty-nine – he twenty-four. The marriage was strongly disapproved of by Lady Elizabeth, his mother and, apparently, by the Bedfordshire gentry. It was remarked that while Judith was mistress of Southill 'the gravel was seldom disturbed' by callers.[5]

William had wanted to follow his late father as MP for Bedford but, at the age of twenty had been too young to seek election. So his brother-in-law, Captain William Waldegrave, agreed to 'keep the seat warm for him' and in 1818 Whitbread was duly elected. He sat in the House of Commons for seventeen years without ever speaking in that chamber which had resounded to literally hundreds of speeches from his father. However, he supported with his vote many of the causes previously espoused by his father – Catholic emancipation, the Reform Bill, the new Poor Law and the final abolition of slavery in 1833. He was renowned for his probity and aversion to anything that smacked of bribery. In the 1835 election campaign, when the rising tide of Conservatism was to sweep him from the House, it was suggested that he might have a chance of success by being somewhat free with the financial inducements that were so often a feature of elections in those days. Someone called out, 'Twenty pounds will do it, Mr Whitbread.' 'Not twenty pence,' he replied dryly.[6]

On leaving the House he threw himself into Bedfordshire life. As High Sheriff of the county in 1837, one of his duties was to attend the proclamation of Queen Victoria as Queen. Country sports also played a large part in his life. Both he and his brother were keen shots and in 1820 William's game book records him partridge shooting on no fewer than thirteen days in September alone, with bags of up to twenty-five brace being accounted for. In 1865 Southill was the scene of the country's first-ever Field Trial for dogs.[7]

Since their youth, William and his brother had hunted with the Oakley. Hare coursing took place on the Cardington fields, and the Cardington Coursing Club presented him with a magnificent silver teapot and water jug (still in use today) with the inscription: 'Presented to William Henry Whitbread Esq by the Members of the Cardington Coursing Club as a small acknowledgement for the Kindness he has so liberally extended to them of sporting over his Manors AT CARDINGTON and as a mark of their sincere respect and esteem. April 1836.'[8]

William succeeded his father as Perpetual President of the Bedford Infirmary, a position he was to hold for over fifty years. During this period the number of in-patients grew rapidly (from 290 to 1,444 in the first thirteen years of his presidency) and a fifty-bed fever hospital was opened in 1848.[9] He was also one of the four Bedfordshire representatives on the Committee of Visitors responsible for the building of the Three Counties Lunatic Asylum at Arlesey. Further afield, he was one of the founders of the English (later Royal) Agricultural Society in 1838 and is depicted in the great painting by Richard Ansdell of the meeting of the society in 1842.[10]

But it was for his championing of the railways that William Henry Whitbread is best remembered in Bedfordshire. Historically the first railway in England was that between Stockton and Darlington, which opened in 1825, but this was chiefly a line carrying minerals, and it was the Liverpool and Manchester Railway (1830) which was the first true passenger railway line. Four years later the first turf was cut for the London to Birmingham line, spawning the lines to Bletchley and Leighton Buzzard (1846 and 1848 respectively); these were the first lines to serve Bedfordshire.

William actively supported the plan for the Bedford/Bletchley line as early as 1840, and when a line between Leicester, Bedford and Hitchin was proposed, realising that, between Bedford and Hitchin, one eighth of the land required was in his ownership, he offered the land to the Midland Railway at no more that £70 an acre. The necessary Act of Parliament was passed in 1853, work started in April 1854 and the line was opened in May 1857 amid great rejoicing.

Whitbread had negotiated with the Midland Railway the right to stop trains at Southill and Cardington stations, and, to ensure that this right was preserved, gamekeepers were instructed to ask the stationmasters to stop trains so that a brace of rabbits or pheasants could be placed in the guard's van at Cardington and taken off at Southill, or vice versa.[11]

William also supported the Bedford to Cambridge line in the 1850s and had been Chairman of the Bedford to Northampton Railway, which would open in 1872, four years after his death.[12] His encouragement of the railways is commemorated by an obelisk which stands in Keepers' Warren, close to where the trains ran on leaving Southill station for Shefford. The inscription reads:

> To William Henry Whitbread Esquire For his Zeal and Energy
> in promoting Railways through the County of Bedford. 1864.
> Erected by Public Subscription.

Shortly after the death of Samuel Whitbread II, responsibility for the Brewery passed to William Henry – on his twenty-first birthday, in fact.[13] This inheritance included debts of at least £200,000. It took young William three years to sort out his father's affairs and resulted in the sale of the freeholds and leaseholds of the premises to the brewery in return for a partnership. The managing partners were Michael Bland and John and Joseph Martineau, and neither William Henry nor Samuel Charles (also a partner) took an active part in the running of the company, now called Whitbread, Martineau & Co. The diarist Thomas Creevey has left a record of dining at Chiswell Street in May 1823. 'I really had a most agreeable dinner at Sam Whitbread's brewery on Saturday. We sat down 22, I think. Sam and William both behaved as well as could be... The entertainment of the day to me was going over the brewery after dinner by gas-light. A stable brilliantly illuminated, containing ninety horses worth 50 or 60 guineas apiece upon an average, is a sight to be seen nowhere but in this "tight little island". The beauty and amiability of the horses was quite affecting; such as were lying down we favored with sitting upon – four or five of us upon a horse...'[14]

Another new partner was Charles Shaw-Lefevre, MP, who had married Emma Laura, William's younger sister, in 1817. He was elected Speaker of the House of Commons in 1839, an office he held for eighteen years. He joined the partnership in 1840 and began the tradition of the Speaker's Coach being drawn by Whitbread dray horses on state occasions.[15]

Although William's marriage to Judith seems to have alienated his mother's affections (she left family jewels, plate and pictures to her daughters), the impression given in letters written by Judith between 1823 and 1835 is that of a woman at ease with her position in life and certainly not daunted by moving in political and artistic circles. Turner, Wilkie, Landseer and Chantrey appear to have been friends, sharing the Whitbreads' table and, in Turner's case, being sent by Judith a hare and a brace of pheasants for Christmas in 1837.[16]

The letters also give an insight into life at Southill. In October 1831 she describes a terrible thunderstorm which hit Southill late one afternoon: '…it seemed to collect from every quarter, and speedily burst upon the centre of our Park, passing over in the direction of Biggleswade. Such thunder and lightening [sic] I never beheld, accompanied with Lumps of Ice and hail stones that measured an inch and ½ to 2 inches in diameter. Many of the pieces of Ice were from 3 inches and ½ to five inches in length. All our skylights, 7 in number, came down with a tremendous crash – and instantly the corridors upstairs, which they lighted, were fill'd with Water, Ice and broken glass – a good many of the windows, in the north front of the House, were broken – and all the Glass in the Garden was demolished – a fine crop of Grapes, Melons, and Cucumbers all destroyed – in the garden alone, twelve thousand, six hundred, and ninety six panes of glass were broken – making with those in the House about 14,000.[17]

In October 1834 she writes from their house in Eaton Square: '…Mr Whitbread is gone into Bedfordshire to pay his respects to his pheasants, some of whom I hope to soon send you'.[18]

It is not clear when the marriage began to founder or when William first set eyes on Harriet Macan. As late as January 1838 Turner was thanking William and Judith for their Christmas gift and yet by the end of the following year, on board Waldegrave's ship, William was talking about his 'domestic troubles' and his love for Harriet.[19]

Harriet Sneyd was born in 1796, the daughter of a vicar, and married General Turner Macan of Carriff, County Armagh. Following his death, and that of Judith in June 1845 (she and William had separated in 1840), William and Harriet married in November 1845. The Macans had had two sons – Henry, who followed his father into the priesthood and died at Southill in 1862, and Turner, who lived at Elstow and kept a pack of harriers – and two daughters: Caroline, who married Captain Charles Grey, RN, and Jane, who married the 5th Earl of Antrim. When William was a guest at the Antrims' home, Glenarm Castle, he complained about the hard seats round the dining-room table, vowing not to return until they had been replaced. Later he resolved the matter himself by buying a set of comfortable red leather chairs and, prior to his next visit, shipping them to Glenarm, where they remain to this day.[20] William and Harriet lived happily at Southill together with Harriet's children, whom William treated as his own.

In the nineteenth century most Bedfordshire villages were very impoverished. Houses were timber-framed, plastered with clay and mortar. Many of the houses had no stairs and access to the upper floor was by ladder. There was little or no running water and sanitation was primitive, to say the least. Between 1855 and 1864 William Henry built at least twenty-one cottages in Southill, in Ireland and at Cardington, as well as Gastlings Lodge in the Park. In 1849 he built a new school at Cardington 'at an expence of between £800 and £900, and capable of accommodating 150 boys'. This was followed in 1862 by the Cardington Industrial Schools, giving seven- to seventeen-year-old girls instruction in 'cooking, washing and all the common work of domestic servants'. This experiment was 'first tried by the Misses Whitbread' (i.e. Gertrude and Elizabeth – William's nieces) 'in a cottage at Cardington', according to the Bedfordshire Mercury.[21]

While the Southill gravel may not have been disturbed by callers in Judith's day, William Henry gladly stepped into the breach to rescue the annual holiday of the Bedford Working Men's Institute in July 1865 when it became 'inconvenient to hold the annual fete on the grounds of the President of the Institute (the Rev. R.W.Fitzpatrick)'. Trains brought no fewer than 3,500 people to Southill station, whence they walked via the Home Farm to the House, where 'the most attractive portions of the Mansion were thrown open...the well laid-out gardens and delightful grounds were perambulated...while the excellent Militia Band gratified the ear with enlivening strains of music'. On the archery ground (now the cricket field) various games and dancing took place, and although 'it had been arranged that the Members for the Borough and other gentlemen should address the assemblage, the various games yielded so much amusement that everyone appeared to have forgotten about speech-making until too late'.[22]

So what are we to make of this puzzling, almost enigmatic, man – indolent in his youth, left fatherless and saddled with debt before he was twenty-one, with the responsibilities of the brewery and the estate thrust upon him before he was ready for them; keen to follow in his father's political footsteps but a silent Member of Parliament for seventeen years; maker of a failed first marriage but with passionate love for Harriet and abiding affection for his new family? Following his death in 1867, Harriet installed a new east window in Southill church with the inscription:

> 'He was a father to the poor, and the cause
> which he knew not he searched out.'

Perhaps the last word should be left to the writer of his obituary in the (admittedly Liberal) Bedford Mercury:

[William Henry Whitbread]...lived among his neighbours. Him all men knew – him all could approach. His form and features were better known than those of any man in the County. Every town and village, every road and highway, knew him. And he was always open to receive all from the highest to the lowest who sought his counsel and needed his help... In truth almost all if not all the public works in the County, public buildings, institutions, railways were initiated or supported by this good man.

So let us sum up, as well as we can, his character in a few words. He was generous, kind and honourable – meaning by honourable of strict probity. He had too a clear intellect, and a force and energy of will that none could resist. He of all men that we ever knew was anxious to know what was the right thing to be done. He more than most men could rapidly, as if by instinct, discover the right thing to be done. He of all men that we ever knew when the right thing was discovered, was anxious to get it done; and the energy and zeal with which he worked to achieve it was never exceeded if ever paralleled. No obstacles appalled him. Impossibilities he laughed at. He had a faith and a will that could overthrow mountains.[23]

Samuel Charles Whitbread (1796–1879) attributed to William Bradley 1841
By kind permission of the Trustees of the Southill Chattels Trust

*I*f William Henry Whitbread is best remembered for his championing of the railways, and for representing Bedford in Parliament for 17 years without making a single speech, his younger brother Samuel Charles made his reputation both as a keen fox-hunting man and as an amateur scientist of some renown.

Born barely a year after his brother, Samuel Charles went to Eton at the age of eleven and to St John's, Cambridge, in 1814. He was in Scotland with his brother when he learned of their father's tragic death in 1815. Four years later the two brothers became partners in the brewery, then called Whitbread, Martineau & Company, and in 1820 Samuel Charles followed his brother, father and grandfather into Parliament, being elected the Member for Middlesex.[25] Within a year of taking his seat in the Commons he spoke in a debate on Parliamentary Reform, a cause keenly espoused by his late father. He compared the House of Commons to a woman of bad character, "with whom you might take any liberty but that of telling her of her frailty." In 1823 he spoke during the second reading of the Sale of Game Act, "convinced that the laws respecting game required to be amended" and arguing that the offence of poaching was being encouraged by the very laws which had been enacted to suppress it. He may have had in mind the cruel murder in 1815 of his brother's gamekeeper, Charles Dines, in Four Acres, a wood on the edge of the park at Southill. Returned unopposed in 1826 together with Byng, he retired from Parliament in 1830 on the grounds of health – some said as the result of an accident. Somewhat surprisingly, in 1872, at the age of seventy-six, he was invited by the local Liberal Party to stand as candidate for Bedfordshire, following the succession of Lord Hastings Russell as the 8th Duke of Bedford. Perhaps in view of his age, the Liberals pledged themselves "to Conduct Mr Whitbread's election without any personal Canvass or trouble to him." Samuel

Charles replied, '…if I had been a few years younger [remember, he had retired on the grounds of ill health forty-two years before!], I would not have resisted such an invitation but at my age I should be wrong in accepting a position the Duties I feel unequal to fulfil'.[26]

Described in one of his obituaries as 'the active head of the large brewery business in connection with which the name of Whitbread has been widely known for more than a century', he lived through an interesting period of the company's history, seeing the beginning of ale brewing at Chiswell Street (porter and stout having been the sole products before 1834), together with bottled beer – particularly pale ale, which was to be a landmark in the company's development. As late as 1922 a brewery employee who joined the firm in 1870 remembered Samuel Charles as a "gentleman of the old school, with his shaggy grey hair, white choker round his neck, black coat cut away at the hips, black trousers to his ankles, showing his white stockings and low shoes'.[27]

In 1824 Samuel Charles married Julia Brand, daughter of the 21st Baron Dacre, and described many years later as "one of the most remarkable and charming women of her time'.[27] The following year their daughter Juliana was born; she married Thomas Coke, 2nd Earl of Leicester, giving him four sons and seven daughters before dying at the age of forty-five. Five other children followed, and Samuel Charles would live to see no fewer than twenty-five grandchildren. His beloved Julia died in 1858 and ten years later, having inherited Southill on the death of his brother, he married Lady Mary Stephenson, daughter of the 4th Earl of Albemarle and widow of Henry Stephenson.

Just as his grandfather Samuel Whitbread I had sat down on his seventy-first birthday and written reflections on his life (his thoughts were of a devout nature, confessing his sins, reflecting on time mis-spent and hoping for a glorious Eternity), so did Samuel Charles on the completion of his eightieth year, but with thoughts of a very different kind. 'On this day,' he wrote, '...I have taken a fancy to put upon record some of the events which I witnessed many years ago with the Oakley Hounds.' There follow many pages of anecdotes, described with remarkable accuracy considering he confesses he never kept a Hunting Book. He was evidently a considerable horseman, often being alone in front with hounds, although he was always careful to give his mount the credit for his achievements.

He was only 18 when he took part in what he described as 'the greatest run' of the Oakley Hounds. On 31 January 1815 hounds met at Colworth and ran four hours and thirty-six miles via Stanwick, Raunds and Wellingborough to Market Harborough. Only ten survivors of the field were 'in at the death' with Samuel Charles, including his brother William and Lord Tavistock. 'We all left our hunters at Market Harborough and rode post horses home,' he recorded – a cross-country ride of more than forty miles!

In the 1820s Lord Tavistock gave up hunting for medical reasons and a Mr Grantley Berkeley took on the Mastership. But before the end of his first season a meeting of the Oakley Club, called by Samuel Charles at the request of his brother, passed two resolutions: 'that it is the unanimous opinion of this meeting that the Oakley Country has not been efficiently hunted during the present season' and 'that...it be recommended to Mr Berkeley to engage a huntsman for the remainder of his term.' This was the beginning of a quarrel between Whitbread and Berkeley which culminated with the latter, accompanied by Lord Clanricarde, arriving at the Swan Hotel, Bedford, armed with a pair of Joe Manton duelling pistols. However no blood was shed and Clanricarde wrote to James Duberly, Whitbread's second, that Berkeley 'acknowledges that he is in error in considering Mr Whitbread's conduct with reference to his hunting establishment an interference in his private concerns, and…is ready to withdraw any expressions in his letters that can be construed into threats or to be personally offensive.' Within two years, Berkeley had left the Oakley Country.[29]

In addition to hunting and shooting Samuel Charles found time to serve as a magistrate, Deputy Lieutenant and President of the Bedford Hospital. In 1840, following the passing of the County Police Act, local magistrates, led by Samuel Charles, established a County Police Force: "…one chief constable at a yearly salary of £250 to include a horse: six superintendents, viz: one for each of the six divisions for petty sessions at a yearly salary of £75 each; forty constables at a weekly sum of 19/-'.[30]

Sam Whitbread II had inherited Howard's House in Cardington and it was here that Samuel Charles and Julia lived. They enlarged the house considerably, prompting this comment from a visitor in 1844: 'Mr Whitbread has made Cardington an excellent house within, though outside the new spacious red wings look absurd each side of the old original house…'[31] In the 1840s a small observatory was built in the grounds and Samuel Charles, together with his gardener, kept meticulous records and astronomical and meteorological observations. His 'Fluctuations of barometer, Cardington Observatory, January 1 1846 to December 31 1870' is now held in the National Meteorological Library and Archives. In 1850 he was among the ten founders of what was to become the Royal Meteorological Society, serving as its first President from 1850 to 1852 and again in 1864. By coincidence, three generations of the family of the murdered Southill gamekeeper, Charles Dines, were to become distinguished meteorologists. In 1854 Samuel Charles was elected a Fellow of the Royal Society.[32]

Samuel Charles Whitbread died on 27 May 1879 at his London house in St George's Square, Pimlico. He had been seriously ill for some time, although his death was somewhat sudden; he was buried at Cardington four days later. Commentators on his life, perhaps struggling in view of his short and relatively undistinguished parliamentary career, preferred to praise his son, 'the much-respected Member of Parliament who has represented Bedford since 1852', and his father, 'the celebrated politician with whose name and services every one who honours political capacity and integrity is, or ought to be, familiar'.[3]

At least the Vicar of Cardington, the Rev. Edward Hillier, in his Whitsun sermon on the day following Whitbread's funeral, managed to find words of tribute to Samuel Charles as landowner:

> To the holder of a large estate the power of promoting the good of all the residents on it is the means of deriving the purest and noblest happiness from the possession of the estate. Such a man, with the spirit of Christ in his heart, becomes of service to many private persons, becomes of service to the public interest of the State, becomes a beneficent agent in carrying on the work of human progress and blessedness for which the Son of God came. When he departs this life he leaves behind him many to cherish his memory with gratitude both to him and to God; and the same spirit that has animated him in his life on earth will make him still at one with God in the blessedness of the life to come.[34]

Samuel Whitbread III (1830–1915) by George Richmond RA, 1860
By kind permission of the Trustees of the Southill Chattels Trust

Chapter Five

SAMUEL WHITBREAD III

(1830–1915)

While it is true that neither of the two sons of the great Whig Samuel Whitbread II distinguished themselves in Parliament, his grandson, the third Samuel, restored the family's political reputation.

Born at Cardington in 1830, he was educated at Rugby and Trinity College, Cambridge, after which he spent a short period as private secretary to his cousin Sir George Grey, then Home Secretary. In 1855 he married Lady Isabella Pelham, daughter of the 3rd Earl of Chichester. Following their wedding at St Peter's Eaton Square, Lady Chichester wrote to her daughter that Sam 'always seems so considerate and kind... I am sure you could not have married a nicer or more delightful person.'[1] They had three sons – Samuel Howard (known as Howard), Henry William (Harry) and Francis Pelham (Frank) – and a daughter, Maud.

Like his father, uncle and grandfather before him, Sam entered Parliament while still in his early twenties, being elected one of the two Members for Bedford (up until the 1885 Reform Act, Bedford returned two Members). He sat continuously in Parliament for the next forty-three years, fighting ten General Elections and one by-election without being defeated.[2] At the age of twenty-nine he was appointed Civil Lord of the Admiralty by Lord Palmerston. As the First Lord was the Duke of Somerset, Whitbread was effectively the Navy's spokesman in the Commons. He was much liked both by the Navy men and by the Admiralty Civil Servants; however, this early promise of success was to be short-lived, for he appears to have suffered some kind of breakdown in 1863 and resigned his office, returning to the backbenches where he remained for the rest of his parliamentary life.[3] His son Samuel Howard Whitbread refers enigmatically to '...a super-sense of conscientious duty...a severe strain from over-work, mysterious sea voyage – resignation of office and – last, but by no means least – doctor's orders for a long autumn holiday in Scotland'.[4]

And so it was that Sam's breakdown led to an almost unbroken series of annual holidays in Scotland, first at Killilan in Ross-shire in 1863, and then for twenty-eight years at Loch Assynt in Sutherland – a tradition followed by four succeeding generations of Whitbreads. In fact Sam Whitbread had been taking shooting and fishing in Scotland since at least 1858 – at Largs, with his Bedford friend and Liberal colleague Thomas Barnard. But in 1866 he found Loch Assynt, where he shot grouse on Elphine and Ledmore, fished the Inver and shot seven stags. Because there was no suitable lodge for himself, his family and friends, he based himself on his yacht *Gondola*, moored at Lochinver. In 1867 he built Assynt Lodge, a sizeable house costing more than £2,000, on what was described by the Duke of Sutherland's factor as 'one of the best and most picturesque positions for a house in this district'. The Lodge still stands, and with it the murals drawn in charcoal on the walls of the smoking room by the 7th Viscount Powerscourt in 1870. One of them depicts a fisherman with a ghillie and has the initials S.W. and D.M. written below – Sam Whitbread and Duncan MacLeod.[5]

But just because Sam III was out of office we need not assume that he was out of politics. Quite the opposite, in fact. For the next thirty-two years he was actively faithful to the Liberal cause, supporting Gladstone as party leader in succession to Palmerston and during his four terms as Prime Minister. He spoke out in favour of free trade and of Home Rule for Ireland. In 1878 he opened the debate in the Commons on the second Afghan war. Just as his grandfather, Sam Whitbread II, had strongly opposed war with Napoleon, so Sam III fiercely attacked the Government in words which might have been used against the Labour Government 125 years later over the decision to invade Iraq. His charge against the Government was:

> That they had adopted a new policy in India against the advice of every officer of experience who had served in the Punjab, and of everyone who was entitled to form an opinion on the subject; that they had attempted to carry out that policy by threats and by language unworthy of a British Government; that they had concealed it from Parliament and from the country because it was only by concealing it that it could be carried out; and further, that having a cause of complaint against the strong, they had fastened a quarrel on the weak, and had thereby brought us into a serious war in order to atone for the blunders of their administration.[6]

After a debate lasting several days, the Liberal motion of censure was finally defeated by 328 votes to 227 – a Government majority of 101.

Described as 'one of the masters of the art of parliamentary speaking' Sam Whitbread also had a reputation 'for knowing more than anyone except the Speaker of the forms and regulations of the House'. He was one of the most influential of the backbenchers but declined all offers of ministerial posts.[7]

In 1868 Gladstone wanted him to become Secretary to the Admiralty. Twelve years later Sam declined the presidency of the Board of Trade, a Cabinet post. Twice offered the Speakership of the House of Commons, he also refused Gladstone's invitation to become a Privy Councillor. Whitbread's reply sums up his attitude to these offers. 'It seems to me,' he wrote, 'that an independent member of Parliament, especially in times of political difficulty like those through which we are passing, has less chance of being useful if he is seen to be accepting for himself marks of distinction which fall quite naturally and properly to those who have borne the burthen of Official life. I do not presume to judge for others, but for myself I hold this view strongly.'[8]

In 1885 Gladstone became aware that, since Queen Victoria's accession to the throne in 1837, only seven new peers had been created from commercial or industrial backgrounds and that all but one of these had public service connections. He determined to seek peerages for Sam Whitbread and Sam Morley, but there was opposition from the Queen – and in any case both Sams refused to accept the offer.[9]

The final offer did in fact come from the Palace in 1902, shortly before the Coronation of King Edward VII. The King decided to confer peerages on two Members of Parliament, one from either side of the House. One of the Liberal names was that of Sam Whitbread, but he 'respectfully petitioned that he should not be made a peer', pleading, it is said, a family tradition...[10]

During his long years on the backbenches, Samuel Whitbread did much to bring about the beginnings of what we now know as local government. Together with William Rathbone he employed a barrister to frame an ideal Local Government Bill, which in time became the Local Government Act of 1888, creating the first county councils.

Appropriately, Sam himself was a member of the first Bedfordshire County Council, serving as a county alderman until 1913.

As one of the Bedford Members of Parliament, Whitbread in 1852 became a trustee of the Harpur Trust, which had been experiencing severe financial difficulties. Some years later the Trust ran into another crisis, when the Endowed Schools Commission was determined to divert the Trust's endowments from its original purposes and indeed threatened to confiscate the charitable endowments. It was decided to petition both Houses of Parliament, and we are told that 'Mr Whitbread's moderating influence was undoubtedly one of the chief factors in the ultimate production of a Scheme that was acceptable to the town and to Parliament; the danger of the town being deprived of the endowment was averted, the existing Schools were saved, and provision was made for establishing two secondary schools for girls, besides enabling elementary education to be given for several years without a School Board.'[11]

Whitbread served as Chairman of the Harpur Trust from 1873 to 1895, a period when both the High School and the Girls' Modern School (later Dame Alice Harpur School) were built. During the 1892 general election campaign the Bedfordshire Times published a leading article entitled 'Mr Whitbread's qualifications'.[12]

> Some persons, who ought to – and perhaps do – know better, have been trying to persuade the working men of Bedford that Mr Whitbread has but few claims on the gratitude of the Bedford people. Old inhabitants know better; but new residents and the younger artisans may be misled by these industriously circulated misrepresentations.
>
> Nothing could be more false than these misrepresentations.

To take first Mr Whitbread's action with relation to the Harpur Charity. A study of the many debates and controversies that took place while the present Scheme was being drawn up would show that no man did more than Mr Whitbread to keep the Charity in Bedford – from which there was a danger of it being taken – and to spread the enjoyment of it fairly over all classes of the local population. The Scheme as it came out of Mr Whitbread's hands steered clear on the one hand of making the endowment a pauperising and demoralising charity, and on the other hand of depriving the poor of its aid. The Scheme has given us some of the best Elementary Schools in the kingdom without a rate; and a system of Higher Schools which are the envy of the country, and have made Bedford the unequalled educational residential town of the Midlands. In the surprising prosperity of Bedford – a prosperity due entirely to the Scheme of which Mr Whitbread was the chief adviser – the working classes have shared equally with others...[13]

In addition, Samuel Whitbread was for many years President of the Bedford County Hospital, following in the footsteps of his father and uncle. He gave £5,000 towards the building of the new hospital and a further £5,000 in memory of his daughter Maud who died in 1898 aged just thirty-nine. He also bought Rye Close, a private house adjoining the hospital, 'to prevent undesirable development'. The house was let to the War Office for occupation by soldiers stationed in Bedford; after the Great War his son Samuel Howard Whitbread presented it to the hospital for use as a private nursing home.[14]

Away from Parliament and Bedford, Sam Whitbread inherited Southill from his father in 1879. He was a great builder. Between 1882 and 1900 he built at least thirty-eight cottages (which bear his initials to this day) as well as five substantial farmhouses. He was responsible for rebuilding Elstow and Cardington churches, the latter on a scale which would accommodate what he foresaw as Bedford's expansion to the south-east (in fact the expansion took place to the north and west of the town and only in the last years of the twentieth century was there any significant development in the Cardington area). He was Chairman of Southill Parish Council from its formation until his death in 1915. He also presented to the local water board the Whitbread well in Biggleswade, which provided water to twenty-five parishes with a population of more than 30,000.[15]

During his time at Southill much of the shooting on the estate was let, the tenant of Cardington being General Mills, Samuel Charles Whitbread's son-in-law. The main pheasant shooting took place in the park, Keeper's Warren, Exeter Wood and Warden Great and Little Woods. From the 1880s up to the Great War, pheasant shooting took on a new significance for country estates, with landowners vying with each other for the prize of luring the Prince of Wales (later King Edward VII) to their shoots with promises of huge bags of pheasants, extravagant food and drink – and pretty ladies. Happily at Southill things were not done on this scale, though the records show a steady increase in the total number of pheasants shot – in 1884: 1,123; in 1911: 4,317. In 1911 (after Samuel Whitbread himself had ceased shooting), on three consecutive days, six guns accounted for 2,270 pheasants.[16]

And what of the brewery in Sam III's day? In 1868 he succeeded his uncle William Henry as a partner and supervised the transformation of the business from a partnership to a limited company in 1889, serving as Chairman until his death. According to *The Times*, though Samuel Whitbread 'did not take an active part in the management, he kept in close touch with the business, and his wide knowledge of affairs and his calm and wise judgment caused his decision on any important matter to be accepted with unquestioning confidence by all who were associated with him'.

Nevertheless this was a period of dramatic expansion for Whitbread & Co. Between 1891 and 1902 five brewery businesses were acquired, with brewing capacity of 110,000 barrels; the value of the company's licensed property rose from £26,000 in 1887 to £2 million in 1907. This period also saw a huge increase in the demand for bottled beer, with production from Chiswell Street rising from 381,00 barrels in 1890 to 778,000 in 1905. No fewer than forty-nine new depots and stores were opened between 1891 and 1914 and there was 'scarcely a town or village in the British Isles where our bottled beers are not readily obtainable'.[17]

In 1892 Samuel Whitbread fought what was to be his last general election. His opponent was Guy Pym, a Conservative from a long-established and distinguished local family, and it was suggested that Mr Gladstone might stop at Bedford on his way north and speak in Sam's favour. The Prime Minister politely declined, saying that any speech he made during the election campaign 'must be addressed to Great Britain rather than to Bedford'. However he did write to the Chairman of the Bedford Liberal Association:

... Honours of every kind – in the ordinary sense – have again and again been not only offered to but pressed upon Mr Whitbread, simply in consideration of his high character and his great abilities.[18]

He has, I think, during thirty or more years uniformly thrust them aside, and has given the undivided force of that character and of those abilities, neither easily to be matched, and both backed by indefatigable zeal, to the disinterested service of his constituents and his country.

Without undervaluing others and without fear of giving them offence, I ask where is the man occupying in similar circumstances a place on the benches of the House of Commons, who can be compared to Mr Whitbread?

And thus it is that now for a lengthened period a peculiar honour has been earned by Bedford.

On the grounds to which I have summarily referred, Mr Whitbread has long enjoyed, and continues to enjoy, in that much divided Assembly, not only an universal respect and regard, but within limits, I will say an universal confidence; and strange indeed it would be were it now to appear, under such circumstances, that he had lost the confidence of his constituents, who have so long supported him to their own honour not less than his.

Whitbread was returned to Parliament with a majority of 128 (his majority at the previous election had been only 23, so perhaps Gladstone's verbose and convoluted letter of support had had the desired effect). However, only two years later he announced his intention to retire from the House.[19] He wrote to his agent, proudly referring to his 'nearly forty-two years...and eleven hard-fought contests...a record not easy to rival – hard indeed to beat'. The news was received by the people of Bedford 'with inexpressible sorrow', according to one local newspaper. 'It was well known that the health of our Borough Member had for some time been broken, and that he was suffering from impaired vision and a growing deafness... The last canvass exhausted him so much that he was a long time recovering – if indeed he has yet recovered – from its effects. His long experience has convinced him that a contest can not be effectually fought without a house-to-house canvass; and to this he now feels unequal.'

The following year he retired as Chairman of the Harpur Trust and in 1896 was absent when a full-length portrait of him by John Collier was unveiled at Bedford's Shire Hall (where it hangs to this day). In the words of a local newspaper, 'It was generally admitted that the likeness was faultless, but some thought that the figure gave no idea of Mr Whitbread's stature and was not robust enough.'[20]

In 1900 he took part in his last day's driven shooting at Southill, though he continued to walk the stubbles and hedgerows with his agent and keeper until the 1903/4 season.

Samuel Whitbread made his last political speech in Bedfordshire in 1905. It included words which concisely sum up his political thinking: 'Believe in your principles. If any measure is put before you, try it by the touchstone of liberty, and if it makes for that, go forward without fear.'

Sam's final illness appears to have started in about 1910. His daughter-in-law Madeline referred in her diary to 'Father Sam [having] trouble with his bladder'. In 1913 she describes his 'gentle decline... He walks, a vastly tall bowed figure, a grey shawl hanging on his shoulders and a little black skull cap on his head. His kindly blue eyes as bright as ever and his gleaming silver beard beautifully trimmed. He is very old and weak and only walks from one room to another but goes out with her [Lady Isabella] in the pony carriage, a most delicious sight that equipage, 2 fat ponies, a fat short coachman and footman on the box and in the carriage dear father Sam, muffled in his grey coat very bowed but alert and keen and by his side his faithful old wife, very bowed too and always, bless her, bothering him and everyone else about some utterly unimportant trifle'.[21]

His final appearance was in August 1914, when he visited the Southill cricket field in a bath-chair. From then on he was confined to his room, suffering first from heart trouble and finally from bronchitis, to which he succumbed on Christmas Day 1915.[22] An entry in the Estate Game Book records: 'Samuel Whitbread died on Dec 25 1915 and shooting ceased for the remainder of the season.'

He was buried in the churchyard at Southill, the first of the Whitbreads to be laid to rest there.

Samuel Howard Whitbread CB (1858–1944) by Sir Oswald Birley, 1930
By kind permission of the Trustees of the Southill Chattels Trust

Chapter Six

SAMUEL HOWARD WHITBREAD

(1858–1944)

I have always thought of my grandfather Howard Whitbread[1] as something of a reluctant politician. Like most Whitbreads he had a strong feeling of tradition and was conscious of the fact that no fewer than five of his forebears had sat in the House of Commons. However, during his last years as a Member of Parliament he found himself in an impossible situation, due to the conflict of interest between the temperance wing of his party and his inheritance from the brewery.

Howard Whitbread was born in London on 8 January 1858. At the age of five he was taken by his father to pay his respects to the Prime Minister, Lord Palmerston.[2] In his youth Palmerston had frequently had to face, as Secretary at War, the attacks of Samuel Whitbread II, and it is interesting to consider that this child who stood before him in his Piccadilly house was to live to see the House of Commons wrecked by a flying bomb in the Second World War.

At Eton (according to an inscription in a book given to him on leaving the school in 1876) he was, besides being 'heir of noble Whig traditions, an excellent oar, a straight shot, a good singer and a true Eton boy'.[3] It was at Eton that Howard discovered a facility for painting in watercolour and his view of the college from across the river won him the school drawing prize. (This painting hung in the rooms at Eton of both his sons, his grandson and one of his great-grandsons.) His affection for Eton meant that when his sons Simon and Humphrey were there it was he, rather than his wife Madeline, who visited them. From Eton he went to Trinity College, Cambridge, from which he graduated in 1879, 'full of the idealism of Liberal politics', as he later wrote. Gladstone was his hero and it came as something of a shock to learn, after a few months in London, of the 'selfishness, indifference and brutality among men and women whom I had pictured to myself as ever marching shoulder to shoulder with their faces turned towards the light and one common enthusiasm in their bosoms. On the whole I think the women were the worst; but on occasions I heard from men who had been second only to our great chief in my idealism, the most callous and disloyal criticisms of their chief'.[4] Was this the first hint of Howard's political naivety which would dog him during his intermittent political career?

It was not long before his political apprenticeship began. In 1880 his father, who had been Civil Lord of the Admiralty in Palmerston's government, arranged for young Howard to serve as assistant private secretary to Lord Northbrook, the First Lord of the Admiralty. Northbrook had been Governor-General of India in the 1870s and it was probably through him that Howard spent two years in India and Kashmir[5] between 1882 and 1884, where his appetite for the high hills was doubtless developed. He had stalked with his father at Assynt from the age of seventeen and, during his first long vacation from Cambridge in 1877, had visited Norway.[6]

But his political career had to take precedence over his love of stalking, and in 1885 Howard was adopted as the Liberal candidate for Bootle in Lancashire. From the very start of the election campaign questions were asked as to his suitability to represent the Liberal cause, not only on account of his youth and inexperience (he was twenty-seven), but also because his connection with the brewery would alienate the temperance wing of the party. A letter to *The Times* (26 September 1885) refers to '...the most reliable section of the Bootle Liberals [being] the Liberal teetollers. Was it wise, was it kind, was it even fair to them who have loyally worked for and voted with the party in evil days, to put forward as the only possible Liberal candidate the son of a brewer, the descendant of generations of brewers, and the heir of a great and prosperous brewing firm, to swell the ranks of the brewing interest in the House of Commons?' In addition Charles Parnell, the Irish militant, instructed the Irish voters to vote Conservative in order to put pressure on Gladstone (which eventually led to his resignation as Prime Minister).

In the event, Howard was defeated by the Conservative candidate Colonel Sandys by 2,782 votes.[7] A bound volume of press cuttings from the campaign was presented to him 'by his affectionate Liverpool friends, with the firm conviction that whereas "ce n'est pas que le premier pas qui coute", so this fair record is but the first chapter of a true political success.

> In the lexicon of youth, which fate reserves
> For a bright manhood, there is no such word
> As fail'.[8]

Howard spent the next four years on a series of sporting expeditions to the Pyrenees, United States, British Columbia, Siberia and Mongolia.[9] However, in 1892 he was back on the hustings, this time contesting the South Huntingdonshire constituency for the Liberal Party. He was narrowly defeated by the Conservative by a majority of 22. Two months later he was selected as Liberal candidate for South Bedfordshire at a by-election caused by the raising to the peerage of the sitting Member of Parliament, Cyril Flower, who became Lord Battersea.[10]

Once again Howard's brewing interests were to feature in the election campaign. A year earlier, Gladstone had announced what became known as the Newcastle Programme.[11] This was in fact a hotch-potch of measures designed to please various elements of the Liberal Party, including Home Rule for Ireland, Church disestablishment in Wales and Scotland, triennial parliaments, leasehold reform, employers' accident liability and shorter working hours. Tucked into the programme, largely as a sop to the temperance movement, was a pledge to bring in a Bill allowing a local veto on the selling of alcohol. Although it was felt unlikely that such a Bill would ever be passed, the pledge caused problems for Howard Whitbread as a Liberal brewer. The local Liberal Party included a number of supporters of the local veto, especially the temperance movements in Luton and Leighton Buzzard. On the other hand, there was a vocal and influential Licensed Victuallers lobby which opposed the local veto.

At an election meeting in Luton, Howard attacked a Colonel Tyler who had chaired a meeting in support of the Tory candidate, Colonel Duke. 'One of the most extraordinary characteristics of Tory speeches,' he said, 'is that they are everlastingly nailing their colours to the mast, and placing their tails between their legs and leaving their colours to look after themselves. The whole path of history is marked out by a series of barren poles from which hang the tattered remnants of the colours which the Tories have nailed to the mast.'

On polling day Howard was elected with a much-reduced

majority, down from 1,022 to 242 votes.[12] Howard had supported the Newcastle Programme. To his dismay the local veto was included in the Government's Liquor Traffic (Local Control) Bill, which Howard described as 'a prohibition bill, pure and simple'. He suggested that the temperance movement should consider whether its benefits were not outweighed by the objections to be urged against it.[13] However he pledged himself to support the Bill at second reading, much to the dismay of the Licensed Victuallers.[14]

Samuel Whitbread III had decided not to stand for re-election at the 1895 general election after representing Bedford for more than forty years, and the Bedford Liberal Association cast about for a successor. As a Whitbread and a sitting Member of Parliament, Howard was obviously a strong candidate. However, as he himself noted, there were doubts being expressed about his suitability. 'Our future Member shall not, as Sam Whitbread, refuse to interest himself in matters of local interest...' 'Howard Whitbread is not as good a man as his father...'[15] And on a night of Tory gains nationally, Howard was defeated by Guy Pym, a cousin of Francis Pym of The Hasells.[16]

As was his habit in defeat, Howard's focus shifted from politics to the high hills and between 1897 and 1903 he travelled widely – to Spain and Sardinia, to the Caucasus, India and Japan, to the Nile, Newfoundland and Austria.[17] It was during his journey up the Nile in early 1901 that he came to the attention of his future bride, Madeline Bourke.

Madeline's father Edward was the sixth son of the 5th Earl of Mayo. The eldest brother, Richard, the 6th Earl, was Governor-General of India and was assassinated in 1872 while on an official visit to the Anderman Islands. Madeline's mother, Emma Hatch, was a noted beauty and a great favourite of the Prince of Wales, later Edward VII, who addressed her in his letters as 'my dearest little one'.[18] She met

Edward Bourke while he was serving in India as his brother's military secretary. He died relatively young and in 1908 Emma married the 5th Earl of Clarendon, who had been Lord-in-waiting to Queen Victoria and later Lord Chamberlain to Edward VII.

Howard's companion on the Nile expedition was Charles Adeane, whose wife invited Madeline to stay in early 1901. Madeline later recalled letters from both Charles and Howard being read out 'and Howard's charm and merits poured into my ears'. Later that year they met. '[Howard] was beautiful to look at – a fine strong figure – great dignity – great charm'.[19] But it took two years for him to propose and, after a brief engagement, they married in 1904.

Whether or not Madeline had ideas about becoming a leading London political hostess, Howard's parliamentary career would end after just five years of marriage. In 1906 he fought South Huntingdonshire for the Liberals, turning a Conservative majority of 280 into a Liberal one of 360 (the 1900 election, at the height of the Boer War, had been nationally a triumph for the Tories; 1906 produced a Liberal landslide).[20] The combination of a sizeable Liberal majority in Parliament and the radical Lloyd George as Chancellor of the Exchequer in Asquith's Government in 1908 caused Howard to feel increasingly unhappy in the party he and his forebears had served for so long. As had happened throughout his political career, he found himself caught in the middle between the licensees, who looked to him as a Whitbread to protect their interests, and the temperance movement, which looked to him as a Liberal to espouse its cause. The crunch came with the 1908 Licensing Bill, described by Madeline as 'that dreadful bugbear of our personal and political life'.[21]

Although Asquith had given an assurance that the Government would not introduce confiscatory legislation, he added that this assurance was given 'without prejudice to the point at which interference ends and confiscatory action begins'. In a speech during the debate on the Licensing Bill, Howard gave an example showing that the balance between the compensation levy paid by the brewery and the actual compensation paid worked against the shareholder's interests. The shareholder 'would continue to pay 1 per cent on his shares by way of insurance and in return for a small fraction of his property. Then, if he survived so far, subject to local vote, he would be invited to compete at auction for the recovery of something that yesterday was his own property, but since had been resumed by the State. The whole process resembled cutting off a man's legs and then punishing him [because] he had no visible means of support. That seemed to pass the point where legitimate interference ended and confiscatory action began.'

Howard, together with seven other Liberals, voted against the Government on the second reading of the Bill. This action did not enamour him to his constituency association. Madeline was bitter because, with Asquith as Prime Minister, Howard could have hoped for a post in the Government. 'I have to pocket my ambitions,' she wrote. She blamed 'that dreadful Whitbread modesty and the fact that Howard remains solemnly in his own path and won't push'. She felt that he would probably retire from politics at the end of 1908, 'a cold douche to my hopes. He is completely out of sympathy with the Party. He is a Liberal – a Whig… [but] they are crushed out between Radicals and Unionists.'

The following year he did indeed decide not to stand again. 'I boil with resentment,' wrote Madeline. 'He has almost become a Unionist from anger with his Party.' In fact, in the general election of 1910, he voted Unionist for the first time.

Samuel Howard Whitbread's political career had been a series of triumphs and disappointments. Perhaps he lacked the common touch. Certainly Madeline commented that 'he does not do popular things like shaking hands and remembering which child had had the measles'. Perhaps he was politically naïve. 'He always thinks people are actuated by the same splendid, aloof, broad and noble outlook which is his, and never will realise that Asquith, though possessed of a great brain, has no noble aspirations'.[22]

In parallel with his political career, Howard Whitbread devoted much time and energy to Bedfordshire affairs. A magistrate since 1885, he served on the County Council from 1892 to 1936 and was Chairman of the County Education Committee for thirty-four years from its inception in 1903. His retirement from Parliament made him eligible to become Lord-Lieutenant on the death of Lord St John of Bletsoe in 1912, and Chairman of Quarter Sessions until 1915. He also chaired the Standing Joint Committee for thirty-three years.[23]

Though too old to serve in the Great War, as Lord-Lieutenant Howard had a crucial role in recruiting in the County. In the early months of the war he visited most of the villages, encouraging volunteers. He was active on behalf of the Bedfordshire Yeomanry, saturating the War Office with letters of complaint if he felt that the Yeomanry was not receiving the attention it deserved. Once, when the soldiers were issued with grey cotton cord trousers instead of the usual khaki, he protested, 'I cannot allow the Bedfordshire Yeomanry, the descendants of the Duke of Manchester's Light Horse, to be turned out like the crew of a tramp steamer who have just been paid off in Rotherhithe.'

Howard's long record of service to Bedfordshire was recognised in 1930 when the County Council and Magistracy presented 'to the people of Bedfordshire' a portrait of him by Oswald Birley. Six years later his retirement as Lord-Lieutenant after twenty-three years was marked by a ceremony at the Shire Hall at which a silver tray and two silver cups with covers were presented to him. The Chairman of the County Council, Sir Thomas Keens, quoted Carlyle's words: 'The history of any country is the biography of a few great men,' and concluded by paraphrasing Dr Johnson in saying, 'Doubtless God might have created a finer family than the Whitbreads, but doubtless, Sir, God never did.' It is not recorded what impact this hyperbole had on the ever-modest Howard.[24]

But there was another, less public, side to Howard's character – his love of the high hills and the pursuit of the deer and other species that lived among them. We have seen how, following defeats in the elections at Bootle in 1885 and Bedford in 1895, he turned to the wild places for solace. He was introduced to the hills by his father, who, following some kind of breakdown in 1863, was advised to take a long holiday in Scotland. This resulted in his taking a long lease of the Assynt and Inchnadamph shooting in the north-west Highlands. Here Howard stalked on and off for eighteen years, in between expeditions to Norway, India, Spain, Canada, Siberia, Mongolia and Sardinia, and in his stalking journal for 1891 he describes leaving Assynt for the last time with a heavy heart.

I do not hold with nursing grief and I have left little bits of my heart on too many hilltops in different parts of the world to be able to swear allegiance to Assynt, but all the same I have something of the same long ache of pain that went with one after leaving Eton. I learned to love stalking and the hill life on these hills, and in Smith and Johnny and poor old Duncan – dead now – I have had friends with whom existed relations of a unique and wholly delightful kind. Never altering; left out of sight – almost out of mind – for ten months out of the twelve, each autumn the old terms were taken up where they were left the year before without fail and without change. It is an affection which makes no demands and has no offsets; in its great intimacy and solitude it is unlike all others and I have enjoyed it with these men now for nearly twenty years... And the ground too I love, though I am under no lack of sense of its drawbacks from a sporting point of view. These old hills have been my friends for many a long day and though I have sworn at them galore, they have given me some moments of pure joy. Therefore I love the place – love the men – and though I agree to go, I hate the moment of parting.[25]

Later Howard was to embark on hunting expeditions to the Caucasus, India, Japan, the White Nile, Newfoundland, New Brunswick and Transylvania. He was unashamedly what today we would call a trophy hunter. He had a fine collection of heads from all over the world which he hung in the Stone Hall at Southill (by the 1950s some of these were looking decidedly moth-eaten and my father had them removed and dumped in the lake!). However, together with some of his hunting companions Howard was one of the founders of the Society for the Preservation of the Fauna of the Empire (later to become Fauna and Flora International, the oldest conservation body in existence). Following his expedition up the White Nile with Charles Adeane, he presented to Lord Cromer and the Governor-General of the Sudan a 'memorial' (or memorandum) on the game reserve in the Sudan. Howard and his fellow-signatories to the memorial agreed to form a society 'to encourage the protection of the larger game animals within the Empire'. The society was formed in December 1903. Three years later Howard and fifteen members of the society went to see Lord Elgin, the Secretary of State for the Colonies. Howard claimed that there were 'more healthy specimens of the American buffalo [bison] in Bedfordshire than there probably are in the United States', and later in 1906 he put a question to the Under Secretary of State, Winston Churchill, on the need for revenues from game licences and hunting parties in East Africa to be protected by a game rangers' department.[26]

Madeline's attitude to her husband's affinity with the hills and wildernesses is not known, but his only foray overseas after their marriage was to Transylvania (present-day Romania) in 1906. 'For many years,' he wrote, 'the big stag of Eastern Europe had been a beast I had longed to kill. I had an unsuccessful trip after him in the Caucasus [in 1898] and this invitation [from Rhys Williams] seemed to promise a chance of a head which I had often longed for, but never seemed likely to obtain. Madeline urged me to go, and my last scruple being thus overcome, I started on September 8 as far as Ostend.'[27] His companion on this expedition was Tom Barnard, a banker friend who lived at Cople and whose family were leading Bedford Liberals for much of the nineteenth century.

Each year there was an exhibition in Budapest of the best stag heads shot the previous season. The Gold Medal was generally awarded to a head whose antlers measured 48 or 49 inches in length with sixteen to eighteen points. Anything over 40 inches was considered good – 45 and upwards first class and rare. On this trip Howard's best was one of 44½ inches with a width of 40¼ inches, while his host Rhys Williams killed a very splendid stag 52¼ inches in length.

Regular visits to the high hill country were almost a drug to Howard. Shortly before his marriage to Madeline he wrote: 'I suppose the time will come when these steep hills will not attract me so much. Even now at forty-five I find my muscles are not strong enough to do much real rock climbing without the penalty of much exhaustion. But one does not have to climb chimneys every day, and as long as I am not using my hands I think I can go as well as ever, and I love it just as much. I am afraid that a few weeks in a hill country each year have become almost a necessity – they make a new man of me for the rest of the year – and each year I more regret the saying good-bye to the golden birch trees and the wet, dark rocks and the rough clothes and rough weathers, and coming back to stuffy houses and white shirts and Education Committees'.[28]

Madeline cannot have found Howard an easy man to live with. Very bound up with his own affairs – politics, local government, the Brewery (he was Chairman of Whitbread & Co from 1916 until his death in 1944) – he had little time for the social niceties, although deeply attached to his children. As early as 1909 Madeline was wondering whether he would grow to be as grim as his parents when he was older: 'he is already very silent when he is at Southill'. The following year they visited Venice. 'Howard is at his best travelling. He can't worry about the house, whether the furniture is sufficiently polished or not etc. and he is amused and interested all day long. He is very artistic and enjoys everything in his quiet way. And he has got me all to himself, no sisters, mothers, friends to take me from him for a minute. And so under these circumstances he becomes quite delightful to be with and I didn't have to entertain him at all.' She was concerned for his happiness. 'He is happier alone with me than with anyone else, but I have not made him happy... On the other hand he is as physically in love with me as ever, perhaps more so. And he is only happy...only satisfied and contented when I am by him...'

There is no doubt that Madeline missed the social life she enjoyed before her marriage. 'Howard is a wonderfully good husband – but he isn't young and he does not like going out and does not attempt to talk to people he does not like, and those he does like are the dull ones… I am determined to make my home life so far as in my powers lies a success. It is my job and I mean to pull it through… I don't suppose he has any conception how difficult he is to live with… If he likes he can be perfectly charming – but he likes so seldom and is only happy when he has me away from everyone and he can do just what he likes while I trot after him…In every day life I sometimes think I shall go mad. And yet, except for one small row, I have never quarrelled with Howard. I have sometimes howled in my bedroom when I couldn't bear any more, but I have never quarrelled which is a feather in my – perhaps in both our caps.'[29]

When Howard inherited Southill on the death of his father in 1915, he was concerned about his financial situation as 'his father was much less well off than he had been' but Madeline felt that they were 'very rich & I don't want to dash about and spend mints of money'. But some things did have to change and Madeline wrote 'that though things may have been done and customs obtained for 50 years under the beneficent rule of Father Sam & William Henry, yet now Howard & I are here and things must be done our way. Gradually this is filtering through to the people, who doubtless sharply resented the complete ending off of clubs and soup as a right…[30]

'Not that we have parties. No, just family – that's all – for Howard will never enjoy entertaining & from some points of view life here will always be sober & steady & and never rollicking, as I sometimes pine for. But now, with War and Sadness & scarcity everywhere, one asks for nothing but safety. And oh, the blessed woman I am with Howard and my boys at home and oh, how happy this safe, steady life might be with the children frolicking about and the lovely out-of-door life all round us, if only Peace was with us.'

Howard's concern for the future of Southill and the estate is demonstrated by a long letter he wrote to me during the war; in fact the first time I saw it was two years ago when researching material for this chapter.

I am writing this while you are still in the house and my object is to prepare for the possibility of being no longer alive after this war to say my thoughts to you. I have lived here as my home for many years and as a result am deeply attached to this place and to the sort of life I see led here. Consequently my strongest wish for the future of our family is that some comparable life, although almost certainly not an identical one, should continue in this place...

A landed estate is very different from property invested in commercial enterprise. Land necessarily has many men living on it, in many cases deriving their living from it. Therefore the man who runs a landed estate must need have many tenants, farmers, labourers and the like. The consequence of the ownership of much land must bring a man into close relation with many others whose lives he is able to affect for well or ill by his own actions.

Christ taught us much about our duty towards our neighbour. I strongly believe that a landed proprietor is placed by his very circumstances under a peculiar duty to **all** those 'neighbours' who are dependent on his actions...

Money will always be a means to power among men – it is literally the medium by which to obtain the services of others. I believe that the Christian duty of the man with money is to use that power for the benefit of others and only sacrificing that power – by positively giving up all his money – if he is in danger of losing his soul by preferring to use his power principally for his own personal benefit.

It is our duty to help our neighbour. And if we have money (power) and are prepared to use it and direct its power for the benefit of others, it seems to me a sin to throw it away. Such a course of action would be like the overcautious servant who hid his master's talent in the ground and did not use it to increase its potentiality for power...

So I conceive it to be your duty as a rich young man to conserve your capital (your talents) but to use your income with such unselfish wisdom as you may be granted for the benefit of others.

In your position as a landowner, you will be placed in a particularly fortunate position for such unselfish use of your inherited power. And I pray that you will deliberately use that position to the full extent for finding opportunities to help 'your neighbours', particularly those neighbours who, like Lazarus at the gate, are in need...

Howard then goes on to divide the responsibilities and opportunities into the ethical (duty as a landowner), and the aesthetic (how to deal with beautiful possessions), assuming

that you will not be able to live at Southill in the same manner of life as ourselves or previous owners...

Keep the estate as compact as possible. Hang on to the most traditional parts i.e. principally Cardington and Southill. Live in the part you retain...

Look on Southill as a national heritage of which you are trustee for the nation & especially those who can best appreciate it. The rarity of it is its completeness. Try not to diminish it by selling or removing the essential contents. Suggest good criterion is the inventory of 1816 i.e. just when it had been recently completed. Do not restrict contents to those which are particularly 'Regency' but try to leave it complete with all the furnishings, which the inventory shows to have been in it at the time.

Make it as easily visitable as you can, either by the National Trust scheme or make it a museum without a tenant living. Try to leave enough of any sets (e.g. of chairs) to furnish it as for living.[31]

These comments show Howard's deep Christian faith as well as his vision for the future of the house and estate. In some ways they echo the sentiments expressed by the first Samuel Whitbread towards the end of his life, while at the same time suggesting a radical role for the landowner, holding land for the benefit of his tenants rather than seeking to derive income from them to support the running of the house. Of course we must remember that Whitbread & Co. provided Howard with sufficient income not to have to rely solely on estate income to cover the costs of the house and personal staff.

Howard celebrated his eightieth birthday in January 1938 with a shoot at Southill. 'He looked so beautiful in an enormous check suit going out,' noted Madeline. The head keeper, Linford, made a graceful speech saying that 'it was an honour to serve such a lover of sport' and all the beaters cheered and drank his health.

Six years later his final illness began – first in February a bad attack of angina, followed a month later by a heart attack. His doctor said there was no hope and gave him two months to live. Madeline wrote, 'I can't even put into words what I feel, having to go on, knowing that my dear, dearest companion, friend and love was going to leave me.' He rallied in June and was strong enough to sit at an upstairs window to watch a fete in the garden, to the delight of the villagers, who cheered and waved.

But finally, on 29 July 1944, he died with only his devoted Madeline, the doctor and a nurse by his bedside. It added to the tragedy that, due to the war, neither of her two sons could be there to support their mother, who had to face both the funeral at Southill and a packed memorial service in Bedford alone but for her sister, daughter-in-law and two of her grandchildren.

*

When Howard's portrait was presented at the Shire Hall in Bedford in 1930, Lord Ampthill, in words which must have evoked memories of the second and third Samuel Whitbreads, said, 'Nothing is more valuable to any community than the leadership of men who, without thought of personal gain or advancement, give the whole of their energies and abilities to the service of their fellow citizens... We know well that had you so desired you might have gone further afield to gain titles of honour and conspicuous positions in the service of the State, but you preferred to remain plain Mr Whitbread...and to exercise your talents and your influence among your friends and neighbours in the service of this County.'[32]

Replying, Howard said how pleasant it was to have arrived at his time of life and to be made to feel that one had not outstayed one's welcome. 'In your kindness you have decided that I am to hang with my fathers before I sleep with my fathers. I am very proud to think that my likeness should hang upon that wall in the company of the portraits of men belonging to a school of which it has been finely written: "Perhaps as long as there has been a political history in this country there have been certain men of cool, moderate, resolute firmness; not gifted with high imagination, little prone to enthusiastic sentiment, but with a clear view of the next step, and a wise determination to take it, a strong conviction that the elements of knowledge are true and a steady belief that this world can be and should be quietly improved."

In quoting from Bagehot, Howard Whitbread stopped short of the final brief sentence, 'These are the Whigs'. But he certainly considered it an honourable epithet. He once wrote of himself, 'By birth, education and conviction I am a Whig, a Protestant and a Puritan.' The disappointment that Howard must have taken to his grave was that the Liberal Party which he and his father had served so loyally should have moved so far from its roots and traditions that he had been forced to 'cross the floor' and vote for the Unionist Party.

Perhaps his great-great-grandfather, the Tory Samuel Whitbread I, would have understood...

Simon Whitbread (1904–1985) by Edward Halliday CBE RP RBA, 1972
By kind permission of the artist's family

Chapter Seven

SIMON WHITBREAD

(1904–85)

Simon Whitbread broke with what had been a long-standing family tradition in not entering Parliament. No fewer than six of his predecessors had followed the road to Westminster, but this was not for Simon. In an interview in 1976 he declared, 'Every morning, when I look in the mirror, I thank God I'm not an MP'.[1] He was, throughout his life, more interested in people than in politics.

He was also the first Whitbread to serve in the Regular Army. It is said that, at the age of six, he saw soldiers from the King's Royal Rifle Corps (the 60th Rifles) at the Coronation of King George V and decided that he wanted to join up when he was old enough.[2]

Simon's childhood was marked by a series of illnesses. Baptised at home for fear of his premature death as a baby, he had his tonsils removed at the age of four and nearly died while at Eton, contracting pneumonia and pleurisy in his final year. Once he had been removed to the sickroom his mother slept in his room (possibly the only woman to have done so in an Eton boy's room – at least at that time).[3]

He was sent away to boarding school at the age of eight – to St Peter's Court, Broadstairs, later evacuated to Tisbury in Wiltshire. While at St Peter's he had his first experience of warfare, when a German plane dropped bombs nearby. 'They did no harm,' he wrote home cheerfully; 'they fell on a girls' school'.[4]

From here he went to Eton in 1918, to Mr Whitworth's house. Towards the end of the summer holidays he received a letter from his cousin Stephen Burroughs, serving in France with the 60th Rifles:

> I've got some time to spare so am taking the opportunity to try and interest you for a few minutes... I wonder when you go back to Eton. You must love being there and you are making many friends I expect. Are you longing to get back for another Term? I remember I was always ready to return after enjoying my holidays. In fact I used to get frightfully cross and selfish and expect everything done for me. I think every boy does who goes to a good School, and is well looked after. But now I often look back and feel I've been a bit of a beast to my Parents and rather short-tempered on occasions, and one doesn't realise what an awful lot ones Parents do for one that may be hard work for them, and consider it their duty to do anything that's possible in this world to give their children happiness. Simon, I don't know why I am preaching this ridiculous sermon to you, as I am not much older than you and Heaven knows I've got enough faults, but it just occurred to me, old boy, that you might be passing through that stage... Lastly, I think out here one can see men's characters in a plainer and truer light than anywhere else, and I have come to the conclusion that an unselfish man is the best and most useful man on earth... Simon, forgive me for boring you for so long, but it's just a passing thought that made me write this letter to you, as I might not have a chance of telling you...

Two months later, on 4 November 1918, Stephen was shot dead taking part in the forcing of the passage of the Sautre Canal. General St Aubyn wrote, 'There is little doubt that the success there finally decided the Germans to make terms'.[5] News of Stephen's death reached his family on Armistice Day, 11 November, as they were hanging out decorations in celebration of the peace...[6]

Eton was followed by Trinity College, Cambridge, where Simon took an ordinary degree in History. On his own admission he 'didn't work hard enough, coasted a bit and probably socialised too much'. Certainly photographs show tennis parties at Southill, point-to-points at Cottenham and Brigstock and hunting with the Fitzwilliam. His coming-of-age in 1925 was celebrated with a party at Southill with 120 guests dancing in the Drawing Room, with bacon and eggs served at 4.15 a.m. There had not been a dance at Southill for more than 100 years and Howard entered into the spirit of the occasion, placing himself at dinner between Margaret Spencer and Diana Sackville-West. The estate celebrations were delayed until the following summer. Eighty farm tenants and their wives sat down to lunch with the usual toasts and speeches. This was followed by a cottage tenants' tea party for 700 in the garden.

Simon was commissioned into the 60th Rifles in 1927, being posted to the 2nd Battalion stationed at Aldershot. The following year he transferred to the 1st Battalion and set sail for India. Between 1928 and 1935 he served first at Lucknow and later at Calcutta and at Mingaladon, near Rangoon in Burma, acting as Battalion Adjutant for three years.[7] On a visit to Burma in 1934, he returned to Calcutta on the first-ever Air Mail flight between Australia and England.[8]

In 1935 he returned to the 2nd Battalion based at Belfast, where the hunting, shooting and social life must have appealed to him. Then it was back to England, first to Aldershot and then to the Rifle Depot at Winchester. While at Aldershot, Simon was invited to shoot in Shropshire by his commanding officer, Colonel Herbert. Here he met and fell in love with the Colonel's eighteen-year-old niece, Helen Trefusis. They soon became engaged, and Helen's mother, Dorothy, wrote to Simon's mother, 'Simon won't find her extravagant as we have always brought her up to know exactly what we had to spend and we have no overdrafts or debts'.[9] Within six months of first meeting they were married at St Paul's, Knightsbridge, on 26 May 1936. The honeymoon was spent in Paris, Vienna and Budapest, but overshadowing their happiness together was the final fatal illness of Simon's sister Joscelyne, who eventually died on 25 September.[10]

The following year their son Samuel Charles was born and Simon retired from the Army to devote himself to Bedfordshire and to Southill, which he had inherited from his father in 1930 (although Howard continued to live there until his death in 1944). But his retirement was to be short-lived. Within two years, war with Germany was declared and Simon was back in uniform, writing with some foreboding to his young wife, 'God only knows how this business will end. Anyway we have had three perfect years and two lovely children [Elizabeth Anne had been born in April 1939]. I am feeling very depressed but trying to be cheerful'.[11]

Simon and Helen lived in a succession of rented houses in Winchester and he was appointed Adjutant to the Rifle Depot. In 1941 he was posted to the 1st Motor Training Battalion, based first at Chiseldon and later at York.

From 1942 to his demobilisation in 1945 Simon held various GSO2 staff appointments with the 1st Army, which took part in Operation Torch. These took him first to Algiers, where the Anglo-American force led by Eisenhower was tasked to remove the Vichy French from North Africa before they fell into Nazi hands. The sea voyage to Algiers as part of a convoy was not without incident. Many years later he recalled, 'we went halfway to the Americas to get there' (presumably to avoid enemy U-boats patrolling close to the European coast). 'It was 3 am when the alarm bells rang and as far as anyone knew the place was stiff with [enemy] submarines. No one told us what was going on. Next morning we learned that one of the ships had "copped it". A long night, that. I felt pretty frightened and lonely. We slept in our clothes and must have stunk to high heaven by the time we reached Algiers'.[12]

His work behind the scenes in Algiers gave him considerable satisfaction. In July 1943 he wrote, 'It is not often given to one to be occupied, if only in a small way, with a large operation' (the largest combined operation ever attempted) 'in the planning stage and then to be present at the initial landing and then to remain to see the whole operation brought to a successful conclusion. It is very satisfactory and very complete'.[13]

Algiers appears to have been at the military and diplomatic crossroads between Europe and the Middle East, and in December 1943 Simon dined with Anthony Eden, Alec Cadogan and John Winant (Foreign Secretary, Under Secretary of State and US Ambassador in London) on their way back from Cairo and Teheran.[14]

Earlier that year Simon was mentioned in dispatches 'in recognition of his gallant and distinguished services in North Africa'. Simon wrote, 'What gallant and distinguished services are referred to I don't know but it is pleasant to know that one has given satisfaction so to speak.'

Although separated from his young family, Simon was very conscious of the quality of his life compared with that of the front-line troops. In April 1944 he wrote to his brother Humphrey from Algiers, 'I am sitting under the fig trees in the garden of a little hotel looking at the sea. Everything is very peaceful here now and the war seems miles away... There is quite a lot of good music which is fun [the previous year he had referred to 'a symphony orchestra of 70 – all sexes and ages'] and an astonishing number of film and stage stars *en passant*. However, the people I find most fun are the locals. M Vannier owns the hotel and is a complete blackguard. However they look after Le Commandant Whitbread as one of their most valued clients and give the best of everything they have to me. I spend a good deal of time in the kitchen discussing life and food with them in execrable French.' Another favourite haunt was the Villa Celeste, where Mme Albert 'treats me like a long-lost son... It is the best restaurant in the neighbourhood. I dine there every Sunday evening and get all sorts of special delicacies that no one else gets'.[15]

However, this relatively privileged way of life did not prevent him from being concerned about Helen. Writing to her from HQ No. 51 Area British North Africa Forces, he thanked her for sending him 200 cigarettes, adding: 'I am rather worried about you being in London during these [air] raids. I hear they have been quite bad. I hope you will keep out of London as much as you can but I suppose if you gave up your job, they would call you up. It is really absurd that I sit in great comfort here with only a semi-blackout, while you have to cower in an icy shelter or basement'.[16]

Simon had also received news of his father's illness and wrote to Helen, 'I am afraid he won't live long but I am glad they are not going to bother him but just let him do what he wants within reason. He has just about reached the end of the road and I hope he just does not wake up one morning.'

Samuel Howard Whitbread died peacefully on 29 July 1944.

Life in Algiers, though pleasant enough, began to bore Simon after a while and he was relieved to move to Italy in late 1944. By March 1945, when he attended a conference in Naples, his thoughts were beginning to turn towards his return home – hopefully by the end of the year. 'I am regarded as old in Army circles [he was forty].[17] His wishes were fulfilled and he returned to his family in August 1945.

Thus Simon retired from the Army for the second time in July 1945, when he was demobilised. His wife Helen, still only twenty-eight, together with the redoubtable Sam Isitt, the agent, had run the estate and farm in his absence. Simon soon settled into Southill. 'We had a lot of ground to make up,' he said in an interview thirty years later. 'Finances were none too easy, but the outlook did not look too bad'.[18]

His skills as an administrator had been put to good use during his years as a staff officer in the Army, and these same skills he now directed to the benefit of Bedfordshire, to the County Council and to Bedford Hospital.

He had been elected to the County Council the year before the outbreak of war, and in 1949 he was elected a County Alderman, filling a vacancy caused by the appointment of Lord Soulbury as Governor General of Ceylon. (A certain number of Aldermen, generally distinguished or long-serving Councillors, were elected by the Council and absolved from the need to fight elections. Apart from in the City of London, Aldermen were abolished in 1974.) Simon served on a number of the Council's committees including Finance, Health, Local Government, Smallholdings, Staffing and Records, as well as representing the Council on the Eastern Divisional Health Committee.[19]

In 1962 he was elected Vice-Chairman of the County Council. The Chairman, Alderman Martell, said that although Simon was also Lord-Lieutenant of the County (having been appointed in 1957), he was being elected Council Vice-Chairman 'as one of us'.[20] Five years later he was elected Chairman, Alderman Martell praising his 'level judgement, fairness and leadership'. Simon anticipated a difficult period of chairmanship. Referring to the Redcliffe Maud Commission on Local Government, he remarked that the whole future of local government was uncertain. 'Local government has always been in the melting pot,' he said. 'The trouble is, so little comes out of it.'[21]

Within three months of taking the chair, Simon Whitbread was faced with a highly controversial issue. In 1963 the County Council had taken the decision to build a new County Hall, having outgrown the old Victorian Shire Hall in St Paul's Square in Bedford. The original estimate of the cost was £1.5 million, but by 1967 this had doubled to £3 million. One of the leading Councillors, Sir Frank Markham, proposed that the revised estimate should not be approved until more financial controls had been established. 'There has been a combination of errors, negligence and possibly real incompetence,' he said.[22]

After a debate lasting an hour and a half, Markham's proposal was heavily defeated. However, the issue rumbled on for several years, and in 1968 the Buildings Committee considered issuing writs for libel against Markham and his group for remarks made about the competence of the County Architects' Department and the Clerk of the County Council. After consulting counsel the Committee, including Simon, felt that, rather than sue, the Clerk should write to the group demanding an apology .[23]

Simon's prediction that he would have a difficult period as Chairman was amply fulfilled, but his personal authority and experience stood him in good stead, and when he retired in 1969 due to ill health, tributes were paid to his service to the Council and a resolution was passed unanimously 'that this Council place on record their appreciation of the long and valuable services rendered to the Council and to the County by Alderman Whitbread since he was first elected a member of the Council in November 1938'. Many councillors spoke in support of the resolution, their tributes taking up an hour and a half of the meeting.[24]

Alongside his County Council work, Simon Whitbread took a keen interest in Bedford Hospital, and in this respect he was very much following in ancestral footprints.

In 1948 the Ministry of Health took over the Bedford Infirmary and the Workhouse and Simon became Chairman of the Bedford Group Hospital Management Committee. The group included, besides Bedford North and South Wing hospitals, sanatoriums at Moggerhanger and Aspley Heath, Homewood and Edgbury convalescent homes, isolation hospitals at Clapham, Biggleswade and Steppingly and a Hospital for Mental Defectives at Bromham. The headquarters of the group was established at St Peter's Workhouse (the House of Industry that Sam Whitbread II had helped to set up) and the old dining room was made into a committee room.[25]

Simon's workload must have been considerable. As Chairman he was a member of all the sub-committees (Finance and General Purposes and Establishment); monthly House Committees for each hospital when the wards were visited and matters relating to patient and staff welfare were discussed; the Nursing Advisory Committee and the Medical Advisory Sub-Committee, which was replaced by a small Executive Committee in 1955.

Christmas Day would find him touring the wards, with particular interest in the maternity wards, from which he would return to his family at Southill at lunchtime, full of news of any Christmas Day births. Just as in the Army, where he had had a good relationship with his men, so with the hospitals, where he knew everyone from the Matron to the surgeons and nurses and was always quick to counter any criticism of patients' treatment. He felt a personal responsibility for everything that happened in them.[26]

In addition to his commitments in Bedfordshire, Simon Whitbread was a member of the board of management of the Middlesex Hospital (where his great-great-great-grandfather, the first Samuel Whitbread, had founded a cancer ward in the eighteenth century) from 1937 to 1948, when the board was disbanded with the introduction of the National Health Service. He was then a member of the board of governors until 1974 when responsibility for the Middlesex was transferred to Kensington and Chelsea and Westminster Area Health Authority under the reorganisation of the NHS. He was also a member of the General Nursing Council for England and Wales from 1958 to 1965.

Following the family tradition, he was a Director of Whitbread and Company. As a non-executive director he left the day-to-day running of the brewery to his brother-in-law, Bill Whitbread, but he was very active, attending dinners for long-serving members of staff, travelling regularly to South Africa in support of Whitbread's fledgling business there (which, in the event, came to nothing) and helping to entertain at events sponsored by Whitbread such as the Gold Cup at Sandown. In 1951 he and Helen gave a lunch party at Southill for the major European brewers visiting England for the European Brewery Convention held at Brighton.[27]

Bearing in mind Simon's huge workload – from the County Council and Bedford Hospital to the brewery, the Middlesex Hospital and the General Nursing Council – and not forgetting his service to the Bedford Magistrates' Court and his appointment as High Sheriff of Bedfordshire in 1947 and as Lord-Lieutenant from 1957 to 1978 – how did he find time for relaxation?

His father had brought him up to fish, stalk and shoot, taking him salmon fishing on the Spey at Delfur in March 1926 (letters record that Simon caught seven to his father's two). When Simon came home from India on leave in 1930, Howard took Struy Lodge in Strathglass and the family moved north for eight weeks in August and September, taking with them the butler and the chauffeur from Southill. There was grouse shooting, stalking and fishing for Simon, Humphrey and Joscelyne, and tennis on Sundays, as well as golf at Rosemarkie with picnics on the beach.

After the war Simon's brother-in-law, Bill Whitbread, rented Alladale and Deanich in Ross-shire from Lady Ross and this was the start of many years of summer holidays in the Highlands for Simon, Helen and their children. In 1947 Bill bought Letterewe, a 50,000-acre wilderness on Loch Maree in Wester Ross. Every August the two families (Bill had six children, three from Joscelyne and three from Betty Russell, whom he had married in 1941) would descend on Letterewe for trout fishing in the hill lochs and, for the grown-ups, stalking. Once the children were safely back at boarding-school, Simon and Helen would return north for the serious stalking which occupied the last four weeks of the season. Although mainly killing poor specimens, Simon did shoot one or two particularly fine heads, including one in 1957 with an inside span of 32 inches.

Simon shot grouse in Perthshire and partridges and pheasants at Southill, where three keepers were employed. He also shot for several years with a syndicate of friends at Euston in Suffolk.

In 1961 he handed over the Southill estate to his son Samuel Charles, taking advantage of an estate duty concession which allowed 'a gift in consideration of marriage' to be immediately exempt from tax. At Sam's marriage to Jane Hayter at Holy Trinity Brompton on

31 August, following the signing of the register in the vestry, Simon declared, 'Thank God. Now I can be run over by a bus.' He knew that at that moment Southill had passed to the next generation, an obsession inherited from his father (and by his son) for preserving the house and estate intact and out of the hands of the Chancellor of the Exchequer, unlike so many other estates which have had to be broken up or sold off to satisfy the rapacious demands of the Inland Revenue.[28]

Simon and Helen moved to a house at Riseley, north of Bedford (said to be a replica of Cecil Rhodes's house in Africa – also called The Mallowry), and Simon continued to play an active part in Bedfordshire affairs as well as fulfilling his London commitments.

Simon's old age, like his early childhood, was not blessed with good health. As we have seen, he retired from the County Council at the age of sixty-four and as Lord-Lieutenant in 1978, a year short of the normal retirement age of seventy-five. He had celebrated his seventieth birthday in 1974 with a small party at Southill among his children and grandchildren, but within a few years frailty set in and he died peacefully at The Mallowry in August 1985.

Simon Whitbread was a man for whom duty was his guiding star. He was not motivated by ambition or self-glory. Political ideology meant nothing to him and he saw himself as an Independent at a time when local government was becoming increasingly politicised. He loved people and was a gregarious character, being equally at home talking to a duke or a taxi driver. He had a great affection for Southill and must have missed its woods and fields after he left it for Riseley (at the age of only fifty-seven), but he realised that the only way to secure the future of the house and estate was to make a gift of it to his son on marriage.

In short, Simon inherited and enhanced many of the characteristics of his forebears, and the words of his great-great-grandfather Sam

Whitbread II could just as easily have come from Simon's lips: 'I have no object but the public good; I want nothing; I seek nothing...'

AFTERWORD

*H*aving brought our journey through seven centuries of the Whitbread family to the living generations, perhaps this is a good moment to reflect on their characteristics and to question whether or not there is a common thread running through the past generations.

Clearly it is only with the first Samuel Whitbread that we begin to have well-documented accounts of their activities and behaviour, but even in the sixteenth and seventeenth centuries we can begin to see the importance the Whitbreads attach to public service. We can also note their strong sense of place, their reluctance to move from Bedfordshire – in fact it always surprises visitors to Southill to be told that, ever since Norman times, Whitbreads have always lived within six miles of Southill, first in Gravenhurst and Shillington, and later in Cardington before moving to Southill. (This ignores the fact that both the first and second Samuel Whitbreads had houses in Hertfordshire although both were buried in Bedfordshire.)

They were also conspicuously generous, both with their time and their money. Clearly from Sam Whitbread I onwards (and due largely to his industry and prudence) each was a man of considerable wealth and it would be easy to say that they could afford to be generous. But it was the spirit in which they were generous that is almost more impressive than the generosity itself. They accepted that their wealth was in a way God-given and that they had a God-given duty to be generous. There is clear evidence of this in Sam Whitbread I's 'Reflections' and in Samuel Howard's recently discovered letter to his grandson.

We must also remember that in the eighteenth and nineteenth centuries the role of the State, both in taxation and in public funding, was very different from what it is today. It was understood that men of means provided hospitals and libraries, even roads and bridges in their neighbourhoods, and that the Treasury allowed them to keep enough of their income to enable them to do so.

It would be easy to assume that each of the Whitbreads was a paragon of virtue. This is because what was written about them, both during their lifetime and after, was on the whole complimentary, sometimes eulogistic even (the exact opposite, in fact, of Shakespeare's 'the evil that men do lives after them, the good is oft interred with their bones'). But if this is the impression these chapters leave, then they are nothing but an exercise in smugness and, even if there is little evidence to support the theory, we must assume that these were normal human beings with all the frailties of humankind. Perhaps they did occasionally drink a little too much, argued with their wives and failed to be good examples to their children. In the words of the Book of Common Prayer which they would have known so well, they '...left undone those things which we ought to have done; and we have done those things which we ought not to have done...'

But the underlying purpose of this book has been not only to set down the story of the Whitbreads over seven centuries for the benefit of my children and grandchildren, but also to hold up our ancestors to them as examples of how life should be lived.

When I was Chairman of Whitbread I had, hanging over the fireplace in the boardroom and immediately above my head, a portrait of Samuel Whitbread I. I remember occasions on which difficult decisions had to be taken, when I would turn and look up into the face of the Founder with the unspoken words, 'What would YOU do?'

Perhaps future Whitbreads, on reading this book, will ask of him the same question.

POSTSCRIPT

*W*hen I gave my talks on the family to local history societies, my father was still alive and I ended the talk with the death of my grandfather, Samuel Howard Whitbread. As I explained at the time, it was as distasteful for me to utter eulogies for the living as it was to speak ill of the dead.

Now that my story has reached the death of my father, I am faced with a similar dilemma. I certainly do not want to embark on an autobiography – not out of any modesty on my part (whenever I hear the word 'modest' I am reminded of Churchill's comment when a colleague of Attlee's described him as 'a very modest man': 'Yes, but then he has a great deal to be modest about') – but from the feeling that my life does not bear comparison with those of my forebears.

But then, for the sake of my children and grandchildren, for whom this book is written, I feel that I cannot leave the story there – hanging in the air, so to speak. And so, on the advice of my family and close friends I shall append a brief outline of my own life, so far...

*

*T*hough I was born in London, my childhood was spent almost entirely at Southill. During the war years, part of the house was used as the Officers' Mess for a detachment of the Royal Army Ordnance Corps, who used the wooded area of the park as a store for every kind of ammunition – shells, mortar bombs, rifle bullets, etc – which were held here before being shipped out for use at the front. The officers were billeted locally, while the other ranks lived in a hutted camp between Gastlings and Gastlings Lodge. The Officers' Mess occupied the ground and first floors, from the Centre Hall through to the Billiard Room and Stone Hall. The Billiard Room was used as the bar, and I soon learned that if I tapped at the window, the obliging Mess Corporal would give me lemonade. This I found very agreeable – that is until my mother was faced with an unexpected and unwelcome Mess bill! A kitchen made of corrugated iron was built out from the Centre Hall steps, its chimney discharging appetising smells below my night-nursery window. The Cook-Sergeant was one Sergeant Livesey, who became a close friend, and when my grandfather died in 1944 it was to Sergeant Livesey that I turned for sympathy, rather than to my mother or grandmother.

In addition to the Army, the house was full of relations and friends of my grandparents – 'evacuees' from the London blitz – who were given temporary or permanent housing for the duration of the war. Among these were our cousin Pamela Hay, with her three daughters and her father, George Burroughes (who had married my grandmother's sister Anne); my grandmother's other sister, Norah Lindsay, who came and went, together with her maid, Daisy; my other grandparents, Robert and Dorothy, and another cousin, Ruth Whitbread.

As the Dining Room was full of furniture from the areas occupied by the Army, the household ate in the housekeeper's sitting-room in the basement, (more recently the Shoot Room) – seldom fewer than a dozen or so – although my sister Liz and I were of course confined to the nursery, three floors above.

The Queen's brother, Michael Bowes Lyon, lived at Gastlings and the King and Queen occasionally spent a weekend there. When we heard they were coming, we stood by the iron gates in front of the house and I was taught to bow as they drove past. My bow was so low that I never even glimpsed the royal couple!

Part of my daily routine consisted of lessons, largely taught by my grandmother Madeline. Subjects included French, scripture, geography, history and music. This stood me in good stead for when I went away to school at the age of eight. However, it also meant that I found lessons at Maidwell relatively easy and could spend more time doing what I enjoyed doing – mainly music and writing. It also must have made me rather precocious (though no one seemed to mind) and before I left, at the age of thirteen, I had written one or two short plays, some blank verse translations of Latin verse and had a 'Country Dance (Opus 1)' published in the *Young Musician* magazine.

It was at about this time that my love of the Highlands was born. In 1945 my uncle Bill Whitbread leased two properties in Ross-shire, Alladale and Deanich, from Lady Ross of Balnagowan. Although I was too young to stalk, there was trout fishing in the hill lochs and, from then on, summer holidays for us meant Scotland. Bill later bought Letterewe, a huge wilderness on Loch Maree, and from 1947 until 1972 we were lucky enough to be invited there almost every summer.

In 1950 I went to Eton, where I did not particularly distinguish myself, although music continued to play a major part in my life. The Dame in my house (Mr How's) was passionate about music. Norah Byron, descended from the poet and a legend in her own time at Eton, would sometimes invite a group of friends to sing madrigals after supper and occasionally, if they were short of a tenor or bass 'the Whit', as she called me, would be dragged from my room in my pyjamas to fill the gap. I sang in the Lower Chapel Choir and the Musical Society, took singing lessons from Mrs Dunhill, widow of the composer Thomas, and occasionally performed in the school concert. I also developed an interest in photography, spending many hours in the Photographic Society's darkroom in the School of Mechanics. I helped found the

Eton College Film Unit, whose 'hidden agenda' was to visit film studios and ogle nubile young starlets like Brigitte Bardot and Shirley Eaton. However, we did produce a comprehensive documentary on the visit to Eton of Emperor Haile Selassie and an adaptation of a short story by de Maupassant, 'Deux Amis', which I wrote and directed. Sport played only a minor part in my Eton life, although I did captain the house cricket side during my last half.

Leaving Eton in 1955, I joined my father's regiment the King's Royal Rifle Corps (60th Rifles) at Winchester to begin my two years' National Service. At the end of twelve weeks' basic training, potential officers attended the War Office Selection Board (WOSB). This consisted of a series of physical tasks including teamwork and leadership, giving a short talk on a subject of one's choice (I chose to speak on Guille farming, an obscure Swiss method involving spraying quantities of liquid manure on to grassland) and an interview. In which of these elements I was found wanting I never discovered, but the end result was that I failed WOSB and returned to Winchester to be told that, even if I did pass later and survived officer training, I would not be eligible for a commission in the regiment, in spite of my father's service. This was a big blow, softened only a little by my promotion from Rifleman to Lance-Corporal ('temporary, acting and unpaid'!).

I did pass WOSB at the second attempt and went to Eaton Hall, near Chester, for officer training. With the 60th now out of the question, I had to decide which regiment to apply to for a commission. I toyed (briefly) with the Royal Fusiliers, who were about to be posted to the Caribbean, but then settled for the Bedfordshire & Hertfordshire Regiment, not a 'fashionable' regiment in any way, but at least my county regiment. This was a decision I never regretted, although I must admit to some surprise when in 2003 I, a failed-WOSB National Service

Officer, was invited to succeed a distinguished general as President of the Regimental Association!

I joined the 1st Battalion in Germany in October 1956. We were stationed just outside the pretty little medieval town of Goslar, near the Harz Mountains. We were within a few miles of the 'Iron Curtain', an electrified fence dividing communist East Germany from the 'free' West. Needless to say, the fence was there to keep the East Germans in rather than the West Germans out, and part of our role was to patrol the fence, mainly as a show of strength. We carried live ammunition on these patrols and sometimes felt that we were very much 'in the front line', although there were never any incidents. At that time the Communists, and particularly the Russians, were a major threat to world peace, and whenever, during our training, 'the enemy' was referred to, we always had in mind the Russians.

The Harz Mountains were a popular skiing area and much of our training took place on skis and in white battledress. As the only subaltern who had any previous experience of skiing, I was appointed battalion skiing officer, which meant that, from the middle of December to the end of February, I skied almost every day. My commanding officer and my company commander were both keen wildfowlers and used to take me up to the Baltic coast near Wilhelmshaven to shoot geese and wild duck.

Military service was followed by Trinity College, Cambridge, to which I was admitted without taking any exams – probably as a result of some effective string-pulling on my behalf by my uncle Humphrey, who had enjoyed a distinguished career at Trinity twenty-five years earlier. Unfortunately my own time at Trinity echoed that of my father rather than my uncle; my father, by his own admission, 'didn't work hard enough, coasted a bit and probably socialised too much'. In his case this resulted in a degree in History; in mine it was a matter of 'leaving without taking a degree' – an American euphemism for being sent down.

Having rejected any idea of a career in Whitbread & Co., I decided to break with many family traditions and become a farmer. My father, very wisely, urged me to get some sort of qualification, fearing that in the future perhaps only those with an agricultural qualification would be allowed to farm the land. Two years' practical experience, one on a Border sheep farm, the other on a dairy and arable farm in Hertfordshire, prepared me for college. At the same time I had fallen in love with Jane Hayter, whose father, Bill, was a noted breeder of Hereford cattle. After a three-month engagement we were married on 31 August 1961, returning from our honeymoon in Italy to start work at the Northamptonshire Institute of Agriculture at Moulton, near Northampton. Most of the other students were aged seventeen or eighteen and I, Robin Kenyon-Slaney and Andrew McCulloch were known as 'the three wise men'. Jane and I rented, for £8 per week, a delightful stone house in the village of Creaton, while my parents prepared to move out of Southill. Halfway through my last term at Moulton there was an outbreak of German measles at the college and, with Jane pregnant with our first child, I withdrew from the college and worked at home from notes kindly supplied by the other two 'wise men'. Free from the distractions of college life, I passed out second and collected a few prizes – a welcome change from my previous failures.

I shall always be grateful for that year at Creaton, with its little garden and roses over the door. It delayed for just the right interval the start of our life together at Southill, which might have been a daunting prospect for a twenty-one-year-old bride. As it was, we moved into Southill in the summer of 1962, at ease with each other and ready to take up the responsibilities of the great house, the garden and the estate, not to mention our young son, Charles, who was to be born in January 1963. My parents moved to a house at Riseley, six miles the other side of Bedford, so that they were not breathing down our necks all the time, but were near enough to come over for lunch and to give advice when we needed it. Their life, since my grandfather died, had been split between Southill and London, and it was nothing for my father to travel to and from London five or six times in a week, pursuing his business interests in London and his many responsibilities in Bedfordshire. Seeing the toll it took on him, I secretly vowed not to do the same – and largely succeeded.

Having settled in to Southill I began to put into practice what I had learned at College and during my two years as a farm pupil. Southill's Home Farm had been hived off from the original home farm during the war in order to provide eggs, butter, cream and milk for the house. A small herd of pedigree Guernseys had been introduced and the farm – all of 70 acres – employed three men! Although I was keen to expand the farm I was unwilling to try to 'buy-out' existing tenants, so I had to wait patiently until they died or went out of business. In time I was able to increase the acreage and at the time of writing, six former tenanted farms have been added to become Whitbread Farms Ltd which now comprises about 3,000 acres – and employs three men.

Soon after we moved into Southill I started getting involved in local politics. Stephen Hastings had been elected as Conservative MP for Mid-Bedfordshire at a by-election in 1960, on the elevation to the Lords of Alan Lennox-Boyd. I was Treasurer, Secretary and later Chairman of the Southill branch and was appointed to the Constituency Executive and Finance and General Purposes Committees.

In 1969 I became Chairman of the Mid-Bedfordshire Constituency

Association, which involved me in attending Tory party conferences. At the Brighton conference in that year I spoke in the agriculture debate. General elections were exciting times and Stephen based himself at Southill for these, particularly while he was in between wives, from 1971 to 1975.

Also in 1969 I was appointed to the Biggleswade bench, and during the next fourteen years I experienced both frustration and fulfilment owing to the vagaries of the criminal justice system. I welcomed the occasional opportunity to sit with a judge in the Crown Court, where both the cases and the advocacy were a step up from the Magistrates' Court.

By now our four children had been born and, on my thirty-fifth birthday in February 1972, I was made a director of Whitbread & Co. At that time, in addition to Bill Whitbread, who had retired as Chairman the previous year, my father, my uncle Humphrey and my cousin Charlie were also members of the board. Whitbread was a family business, with control being exercised through the high-voting 'B' shares, many of which were held by the Whitbread Investment Company whose own shares were largely owned by members of the family and trusts controlled by them. We were one of the relatively few major companies with 'limited voting shares' (the 'A' shares) being the only shares freely traded on the Stock Exchange, while the 'B' shares – each with twenty votes – were closely held by the family. This mechanism, which made us secure against any predatory approach for the company, was not popular in the City and would lead in time to our inability to raise funds by issuing shares (for a major acquisition, for example); the 'B' shares and the Investment Company were eventually abandoned in 1994.

Alex Bennett was Chairman and Charles Tidbury Managing Director, and I soon began to be involved with public relations events and pub openings. Much was made of the fact that I was the seventh generation of the family to be a director. I also of course attended all the board meetings and strategy conferences.

Between 1973 and 1974 I served as High Sheriff of Bedfordshire, at thirty-six one of the youngest in recent times. In retrospect I was too young, as I had not really got to know the County, its issues and personalities; I think I would have done the job better in my forties. What did please me was that my Shrieval year coincided with the 200th anniversary of that of John Howard, the great prison reformer of the eighteenth century. His visit as High Sheriff to Bedford gaol triggered his enquiry into *The State of the Prisons*, which brought to the public notice the appalling conditions in which prisoners were kept, those on remand, for instance, having to pay the gaoler for their board and lodging. I suggested that I might visit Bedford prison but was told that this 'would not be appropriate'. Had I been older, I might have been more insistent.

It had long been my intention to follow my father and grandfather on to the County Council. The politicisation of county councils meant that I would have to stand as a Conservative, but as High Sheriff I was barred from taking part in any political activities. Fortunately, the end of my Shrieval year in April 1974 just gave me time to submit my nomination papers for the Eastcotts Division. I was duly elected and represented the electors of Wilstead, Elstow, Shortstown, Cotton End, Cardington, Cople and Willington from 1974 to 1982. I was elected Chairman of the Leisure Committee, dealing with libraries, arts and recreation, and was given the nickname 'the Gentleman of Leisure' by my Labour opponents. I was a governor of seven lower schools and was frequently asked to attend parish council meetings. These, together with committee and council meetings, kept me pretty busy and, having served two four-year terms and with the prospect in 1982 of a 'hung' Council, I decided it was time to 'make way for an older man' who would be able to give the job more time than I could.

Some of my Conservative friends gained the impression that, having served as Chairman of my Constituency Association and then as a County Councillor, the next step was to become a parliamentary candidate as these were often stepping-stones along that path. It was suggested that I might stand for Mid-Bedfordshire following Stephen Hastings's retirement in 1983. However, thoughts of a parliamentary career were far from my mind. Having seen our own Member of Parliament at close-quarters for five years, I had soon decided that the life of a twentieth-century MP was not for me.

In 1985 my father died, having been in poor health for some time. I cannot say that I knew him well, and it was only after our marriage that I felt I could talk to him as an equal. He was thirty-two when I was born; the war claimed him until I was eight and we were never really close. He was a man of contrasts – puritanical, almost, when it came to duty, never taking the easy way out – and yet enjoying to the full the good things in life, the best hotels, the Bentley, his shooting, stalking and racing. Towards the end, his mind returned to what were probably the happiest days of his life – those spent with his regiment in India.

In a way, ours was a distant relationship. I can remember few times when we were really together – once at Letterewe, the only time I stalked with him. I admired him for his great sense of duty. Twenty-one years as Lord-Lieutenant, the County Council, the hospitals (Bedford and Middlesex), the Bench and the brewery. But it was only in the last few years that I loved him – and then it was a love born out of pity...

Meanwhile events were taking place at Whitbread & Co which were to change my life. By early 1983 it was known that Charles Tidbury would be retiring as Chairman at the end of the year and that the board needed to plan his successor. The non-executive directors, Alex Bennett, Dick Troughton, Tim Colman, Andrew Caldecott, Charlie Whitbread and I, together with the Deputy Chairman Raymond Seymour, Martin Findlay and Robin Farrington, met frequently to discuss what should be done. The decision had already been taken to separate the roles of Chairman and Managing Director and there was no obvious successor among the executive directors. We looked at 'parachuting in' an outsider as Chairman but felt that this ran counter to Whitbread's style and ethos. Eventually I was persuaded, as a last resort and recognising the high risk involved, to succeed Charles as a 'stop-gap' Chairman 'for two or three years', and, at the November board meeting I was appointed Deputy Chairman from January 1984 with a view of taking over as Chairman in August.

This was a huge gamble for the company as, although I had been on the board since 1972, I was not really known either in the City or in the company and I had nothing like the energy of Charles, who appeared to be able to survive on very little sleep whereas I needed my eight hours! It would also mean a huge disruption for Jane and the children as we would have to live in London and deal with the farm and estate at weekends. So I sat down to write thirty-odd letters of resignation from all sorts of organisations in Bedfordshire (not a bad thing, as I had been involved with some of them for far too long!).

Very fortunately from the estate point of view, in 1981 I had appointed Savills to run the estate following the retirement after thirty-three years of Simon Molloy as agent; he had been a tower of strength as well as a good friend to both my father and myself. Mark Egar was appointed as resident agent and brought a modern, focused sharpness to the operation. Largely thanks to him I was awarded the Bledisloe

Gold Medal for Landownership by the Royal Agricultural Society in 1989, which I received from the Queen at the Royal Show. In his report the judge wrote, 'The management of Southill displays an awareness of the many and varied resources of the average agricultural estate and the ability to put these to productive and beneficial use. There is a marked concern for the welfare of those who live on the property and those whose proximity to it inevitably involves them with it in some way or another. There is a willingness to share the resources of the estate with them for the benefit of the whole, but there is no element of the patrician in administration and management.' A tribute indeed to Mark and everyone on the estate.

But, to return to 1984. I had said that I would not do the Whitbread job without Jane's full support and the unanimous agreement of the board and, once I got into the job, I was amazed and somewhat humbled by the huge amount of good will I found wherever I went. I decided to use my seven months as Deputy Chairman to get around the business and the City, and this was time well spent. The press didn't quite know what to make of me. They said (quite reasonably): 'How can a farmer become head of a large international drinks business?' and I was caricatured as a yokel, chewing a straw. I pointed out that in my view any business was about two things – people and money; instead of forty people I would have 30,000 and 'there were a lot more noughts at the end of all the figures'.

In the event, 'two to three years' stretched to eight, partly because after the initial apprehension I began to enjoy the job, and partly because, thanks to all the support I had from the senior management, the company seemed to be going rather well. The share price rose from 164p to 412p, having seen a 'high' of over 500p.

I never wanted to be Chairman; it was, in a way, thrust upon me and having been dealt that hand I played it as well as I could. But underneath it all I had the feeling that I was acting a part, that I was deceiving people into thinking I was a businessman, a captain of industry, a tycoon. In fact I was fooling most of the people, shareholders, the media, even my board colleagues perhaps, most of the time. But after eight years I knew I had given all I had to give to Whitbread and I had found an outstanding successor in Michael Angus. My own verdict on this period in my life was recorded in my diary:

The Board, I think, is more efficient than before, with the agenda better-ordered and papers more succinct. I instituted Board Visits, so that all the directors, executive and non-executive, were forced out into the shops, the pubs, the breweries and the depots. By using head-hunters rather than 'mates' the quality of our non-executive directors has risen considerably. The establishment of Board Committees has meant that strategic and people issues have been given full attention in between Board Meetings.

The Company's relations with the City and the media have been improved – though not as much as I would have liked. I took the gamble of holding meetings for analysts and press twice a year when we announced our results. These could have gone horribly wrong due to my inexperience and lack of knowledge in the early days, but they seemed to work. I had lunches (not enough, again) for our institutional investors as well as presentations for the key family shareholders.

But if I did anything for which I would like to be remembered, it was to raise people's morale and standards. Before, we always talked about the Whitbread way of doing things. I, with much help from others, articulated what we meant by 'The Whitbread

Way' and had it printed in a little booklet for all to read. True, it sometimes rebounded on us when someone was treated in a way he thought unfair or unacceptable. 'Is this what you mean by The Whitbread Way?' was in some cases a justified slap in the face. But it did make people think.

As for me, what have I gained from all this? All in all, it has been a marvellous experience. I have met Princes, Prime Ministers and Presidents as well as a wide selection of business leaders from the discredited Maxwell and Saunders at one extreme to 'good eggs' like Simon Hornby and David Nickson at the other. I have, sometimes happily with Jane, been able to travel the world in great style and comfort. I have earned (I hope earned) a very generous salary which has helped the bank balance and have left with what I also hope is a more than adequate pension. Above all, this mid-life interlude has taught me much about leadership and business; about priorities – sorting out what is important from what is trivial. It has made me a more organised person and perhaps has left me better equipped to make a success of the third stage of my life – as Lord-Lieutenant.

This appointment in 1991 solved a problem for me. How was I to justify retiring as Chairman at the age of fifty-five? 'To spend more time with the family' was a well-worn cliché and never quite convincing, but to say that I was taking on the role of the Queen's representative in Bedfordshire seemed to ring true and I grasped the opportunity with both hands. However, I still had to juggle both jobs for eighteen months, which was not easy.

At the same time, I had other less demanding roles to play. From 1990 to 1992 I was President of the Shire Horse Society and in 1991/2

I served as President of the East of England Agricultural Society. We had a most enjoyable Peterborough Show, with visits from the Queen and Prince Philip, the Duke of Gloucester and Princess Alice, and were kept facing in the right direction by the chief executive, the redoubtable Roy Bird.

Between 1991 and 1993 we carried out some major refurbishments to Southill. The disruption was horrific and we had to move out of the house and into The Kennels for three years. This meant that there was no way in which we could have all the children to stay for Christmas in 1990, so we decided to take them all to Kenya and had the memorable experience of sitting round the camp fire in Samburu on Christmas Eve singing 'In the Bleak Midwinter', followed by a flight on Christmas Day to Nairobi; here, at the Norfolk Hotel, we encountered a coal-black Father Christmas sweating profusely in his crimson outfit complete with beard, ringing a bell and going 'Ho-Ho-Ho'. This turned out to be our last family holiday together, as in August 1991 Charles married and another Jane Whitbread entered the family to great jubilation.

In addition to some significant structural work to the house and stonework repairs, we returned the Drawing Room to its original 1800's colour scheme and the Dining Room was greatly improved by Jane's imaginative scheme – and the discovery that the delicate painted pilasters and overdoors were a glowing marble colour under the cigar-stained varnish that had semi-hidden them for so long.

Upstairs too, Jane worked her magic, with four new bathrooms and some exciting wallpapers, one or two reproduced from old papers found behind mirrors when the house was dismantled, and all with a story and a logic behind them. In spite of the hideous cost, I was glad that we did it, rather than pretending that the problem didn't exist and leaving it, swept under the carpet, for the next generation. The key to the triumph (for triumph it was and is) was Jane, and I know that Southill will stand for a very long time as a monument to her taste, skill and persistence, just as it has been to Henry Holland.

At about this time I started trying to paint watercolours. Both my grandfather Howard and my uncle Humphrey had been skilled sketchers, but I was never inspired at school and it was through collecting, in a modest way, eighteenth- and nineteenth-century watercolours that I became curious about how the great English painters achieved their effects. Without any formal tuition I became more and more frustrated until, in 1994, I met James Fletcher-Watson. It is no exaggeration to say that for me this was a life-changing experience. Here was a gentle man in his eighties, trained as an architect but for most of his life a painter, a follower of Edward Seago and Edward Wesson and with an almost missionary zeal to keep alive the eighteenth- and nineteenth-century watercolour tradition and techniques. He helped and encouraged me, and some of my happiest days were spent each September painting with him and a small band of disciples at Dedham, on the Essex/Suffolk border.

After James retired I tried other tutors, but none of them quite matched his ability to communicate his thoughts and methods, and in 2004 I gathered a small group of painter friends to spend a week painting in the West Highlands at Couldoran, on Loch Kishorn. We called ourselves, rather presumptuously, 'the Couldoran School', and the following year we went to Chateau Ragny in Normandy and, in 2006, to Burgundy.

As I approach my seventieth birthday my thoughts inevitably go to the 'three score years and ten' as man's life expectancy and it always amazes me that in biblical days people looked to seventy as their natural span of life – or did they? It is surely as unlikely that Methuselah lived for 969 years when we are told that the average Roman lived for just twenty-five years; that in medieval times life expectancy had increased to thirty-three, by the nineteenth century to forty-three and in 1911 to fifty. Today, at birth, it is seventy-seven.

But I myself prefer to heed the words of Bernard Baruch, the American financier and Presidential adviser, on his eighty-fifth birthday: 'To me, old age is always fifteen years older than I am'.

Today I find my life revolving around the Lieutenancy and painting. My responsibilities for Southill are largely in Charles's safe hands and it gives me much pleasure to see him, together with his Jane and the children, flourish at Southill, gently putting their own stamp on things. I am beginning to think about retiring from some of the many organisations with which I have been involved for more years than is good for me (and for them), although I still have a further five years to serve as Lord-Lieutenant.

Retirement holds no fears for me as, sadly, it does for some. I never seem to have had time to do many of the things I wanted to do and, with a wonderful wife and family and a delightful house and garden, the years beyond the three score and ten look very inviting, with more time available for Scotland, the grandchildren and painting.

NOTES

Abbreviations

BHRS   Bedfordshire Historical Records Society.

BLARS   Bedfordshire and Luton Archives and Records Service [Record Office.]

CH   Chester Archive at BLARS.

CRT   County Record Office Transcript, reference notes etc kept at BLARS.

DNB   *Dictionary of National Biography*.

L.   Wrest (Lucas) Archive at BLARS.

PCC Prob.   Prerogative Court of Canterbury, Will proved at.

VSB   Vertical Strong Boxes, Southill Muniment Room.

W   Whitbread Archive at BLARS.

W/H   Humphrey Whitbread Archive, held at Southill.

Chapter 1   Early Whitbreads (1282–1727)

1   G. H. Fowler, ed., *A Calendar of the Feet of Fine for Bedfordshire, preserved in the Public Record Office, of the reigns of Richard I, John and Henry III,* BHRS Vol. VI, pp. 179–80, for 1262; G. H. Fowler, *Calendar of Post Mortems I,* BHRS Vol. V, p. 231. The help of late Dr F.G. Emmison over early references to the Whitbreads was greatly appreciated.

2   BLARS ref. L (Jeayes) 380, 383-91; C.A. Torrey, 'The Whitbreads Family of Gravenhurst, Bedfordshire, England,' article in *American Genealogist* No. 127, Vol. 2, No 3. July 1956; P. L Bell, Pedigree of 16-17C Whitbreads, BLARS ref. CRT 190/32.

3   Henry of Hitchin; Brewers' Company Archives, held at Guildhall Library, City of London.

4   Thomas Harcourt, DNB.

5   BLARS ref. L6/63-135, (especially L6/139), Settlement and Sale of Ion; see also L26/557), which maps the property.

6   BLARS ref. W 264-75.

7   F. G. and Margaret Emmison, *The Ship Money Papers of Sir Henry Chester and Sir*

Will. Boteler, 1637–1639, BHRS, Vol. 18.

8 Ross Lee, *Law and Local Society in the time of Charles I: Bedfordshire and the Civil War,* BHRS, Vol. 65.

9 H. G. Tibbutt, ed., *The Letter Books of Sir Samuel Luke, 1644–1645,* BHRS, Vol. 42.

10 ibid., p.121.

11 ibid., p.122.

12 ibid., p.155.

13 H. G Tibbutt, ed., *The Minutes of the First Independent Church (now Bunyan Meeting) 1656–1766,* BHRS, Vol. 55.

14 BLARS, Northill Parish Archive, ref. P10/15.

15 Tibbutt, *Bunyan Meeting,* p.42.

16 ibid., p.46.

17 ibid., p.46–47.

18 ibid., p.68.

19 ibid., p.70.

20 Pedigree of Whitbreads of Southill, drawn up for Samuel Howard Whitbread, 8 January 1938.

21 BLARS, ref. CH 922.

22 W. R. Ward, *English Land Taxes in the Eighteenth Century,* Oxford University Press, 1953; Speech of Samuel Whitbread I in Land Tax Debate reported in *Northampton Mercury,* 12 November 1777; Tallage: 'a capricious levy imposed by the Crown on its manors and owners, or by feudal superiors on tenants of mean or unfree birth' (Arnold-Baker); Scutage: 'shield money replacing feudal military service;' Hidage: 'tax levied on each hide (c 100 acres).'

23 W. M. Wigfield, *Recusancy and Nonconformity in Bedfordshire,* BHRS, Vol. XX.

24 Tibbutt, *Bunyan Meeting* p.129.

25 Will of Oliver Edwards (PCC, Prob.11.723), proved 8 January 1742 [1743].

26 Wills of Philip Read and Elizabeth Whitbread (PCC, Prob.11/752 sig. 28), proved 28 January 1746 [1747].

27 Will of Henry Whitbread (PCC; Prob.11/619 sig. 28), proved 3 January 1727 [1728]. Note also Samuel Whitbread I's Comment: 'My Father had about 300 acres of real Estate but lived as a Gentleman requi[res]t and brought up his children decent & kept his Coach and was Receiver General of the County many years and a remarkable good Character as an honest man.'

Chapter 2   Samuel Whitbread I (1720–96)

1 Dean Rapp, 'Social Mobility in the Eighteenth Century: The Whitbreads of Bedfordshire, 1720–1815', *Economic History Review,* Vol. XXVII, No. 3, August 1974.

2 B. Ritchie, *An Uncommon Brewer: the Story of Whitbread, 1742–1992*, James and James 1992; Samuel Whitbread in *Joshua Reynolds* File at Southill. Memoirs with no indication of original source.

3 Company of Brewers' Archive, commented on by N. B. Redman, 'Samuel Whitbread 1720–1796' in *The Brewer* February 1992

4 Redman, 'Samuel Whitbread 1720–1796'. See also Peter Mathias's *The Brewing Industry in England, 1700–1830*, Cambridge University Press, 1959.

5 Harriot Gordon's *Reminiscences*, in File I of the papers relating to her portrait by Reynolds, Southill Muniment Room, VSB 2, about her father Samuel Whitbread.

6 Redman, 'Samuel Whitbread 1720–1796.'

7 Ibid. p.6; *Peter Pindar*, Printed poem: *Instructions to a Celebrated Laureat; alias The Progress of Curiosity; alias A Birth-Day Ode; alias Mr. Whitbread's Brewhouse,* [satirical view of George III's visit to the Chiswell Street Brewery], 1792 (Whitbread Archive Box 1 at Southill).

8 *Annual Biography and Obituary for the year 1817*, Vol.1, Longman, Hurst, Rees, Orme and Brown, London 1817, (copy at Southill Muniment Room).

9 Notes on individual paintings at Southill are kept at Southill Muniment Room.

10 Mathias, *The Brewing Industry in England*, p. 320.

11 Pedigree of the Whitbreads of Southill, drawn up for Samuel Howard Whitbread, 8 January 1938.

12 Red Book: copies of letters re Samuel Whitbread's attempt to sell the Brewery, 1789–94, VSB 4.

13 Waldegrave Papers, Samuel Whitbread to Harriot Gordon, quoted in Rapp 'Social Mobility'.

14 Quoted in Redman, 'Samuel Whitbread 1720–1796'.

15 Ellen Gibson Wilson, *John Clarkson and the African Adventure.*

16 Rapp, 'Social Mobility'; Red Book of Transcripts of Letters from Samuel Whitbread I to his son, Southill VSB 4.

17 BLARS, ref. L30/ 9/60/195 Polwarth Letter; see also BLARS, ref. W 2205; W 2216-2218.

18 BLARS, ref. CRT 100/27 Transcripts of Hardwicke Manuscripts at the British Library, made by Mary Phillips; *Northamptonshire Mercury*, September 1767– March 1768 (Copies held on Microfilm at BLARS).

19 His campaign against corruption in elections, triggered by his experience at the 1774 Bedford Election; J. Godber *History of Bedford*, p.91 states that at the 1790 Election there were 1,058 voters from the town and 736 from elsewhere; References in the *Northamptonshire Mercury* for October 1774–May 1775. I. R. Christie, *The End of North's Ministry 1780–1782*, London 1958 (see pp. 299ff for Sam's role in the fall of Lord North in March 1782).

20 Harriot Gordon's *Reminiscences.* Thomas Clarkson *History of the Rise, Progress and Accomplishment of the Abolition of the African Slave Trade*, 1808 (copy in Library, Southill); References in *Northamptonshire Mercury*.

21 The background to Samuel Whitbread II's entry into politics is given in Dean Rapp, *Samuel Whitbread 1764–1815,* Garland Publishing Inc New York & London, 1987, pp. 113–123; BLARS, ref. X 202/72, Letter from Matthew Rugeley to Mr Payne of Tempsford Hall, dated 18 June 1790; Sir Denis Le Marchant, *Memoir of John Charles Viscount Althorp, 3rd Earl Spencer*, London 1876.

22 Harriot Gordon's *Reminiscences.*

23 Samuel Whitbread's 'Reflections'.

24 C Bruyn Andrews, ed. *The Torrington Diaries,* Vol. II, p. 109.

25 Harriot Gordon's *Reminiscences.*

26 *Northamptonshire Mercury* for October 1774 and 15 March 1775; Peter Gordon, *The Wakes of Northamptonshire*, Northamptonshire County Council, 1992.

27 Samuel Whitbread's 'Reflections'.

28 Harriot Gordon's *Reminiscences.*

29 ibid.

30 1817 Obituary: 'Towards the completion of the new county jail he left a legacy of £500. He bequeathed £4,000 towards the erection of the Bedford Infirmary; and £4,000 more towards its endowment. In addition to this, he also established a ward for those afflicted with cancers in the Middlesex Hospital.'

31 Samuel Whitbread's 'Reflections'.

Chapter 3   Samuel Whitbread II (1764–1815)

1 Tributes of the public press to the late Mr Samuel Whitbread, Whitbread Archive Box 1, Southill Muniment Room.

2 Roger Fulford, *Samuel Whitbread (1764–1815): A Study in Opposition*, Macmillan, 1967, p.14, quoting Waldegrave papers at Chewton Mendip.

3 ibid. p.16, quoting letter of 25 June 1785, Waldegrave papers at the same.

4 ibid. p. 24 quoting letter of 25 January 1785, Waldegrave papers at the same.

5. N. Redman, 'Samuel Whitbread, 1720–1796', *The Brewer,* February 1992, copy at VSB 4, gives an account of Watts work at the Brewery.

6 Transcripts of love letters from Samuel Whitbread II to Elizabeth Grey, 1787–1788, compiled by Marita Prendy, Archive Box 45, Southill Muniment Room,

7 Sir Denis Le Marchant, *Memoir of John Charles, Viscount Althorp, 3rd Earl Spencer,* London, 1876. The accuracy of this story is strengthened by Samuel Whitbread III's pencil addition, which suggests he thought it was correct. Sam II was possibly insensitive and Sam I was clearly hurt. The background to Samuel Whitbread II's entry into politics is given in *Samuel Whitbread (1764–1815); A Social and Political History* by Dean Rapp, Garland Publishing Inc New York & London, 1987.

8 Fulford, *Samuel Whitbread,* p.51; Dean Rapp *Samuel Whitbread.*

9 Fulford, *Samuel Whitbread* ibid. pp.176–80.

10 Tin box in BLARS, ref. W 1/7000; Fulford *Samuel Whitbread* pp. 115–39.

11 ibid p.140–58; Lord Holland *Memoirs of the Whig Party* Vol. I p. 219.Letter of Samuel Whitbread II to Charles Grey of 7 February 1806, Grey letters at Durham.

12 Fulford, *Samuel Whitbread,* pp. 159–170.

13 Letter to George Tierney, ibid. p 190; quoted in Roberts, *The Whig Party,* 1939.

14 Fulford, *Samuel Whitbread* pp.185, 245 (Scheldt); 201–210 (Mary Ann Clarke).

15 ibid. p. 261–73.

16 ibid. pp. 175–6; Hansard Speech of 5 January 1807.

17 Fulford, *Samuel Whitbread,* p.194; Hansard Speech of 29 February 1808.

18 Fulford, *Samuel Whitbread,* p. 173.

19 P.L. Bell ed. *Southill Estate 1795–1995,* published by S. C. Whitbread, 1994; *Portrait of Southill: A Regency House,* Faber & Faber, 1951; Stephen Deuchar *Paintings, Politics & Porter, Samuel Whitbread and British Art,* Whitbread & Co, 1984; Gervase Jackson-Stops, 'Southill Park, Bedfordshire', *Country Life* of 28 April 1994.

20 Bell, *Southill Estate*; Joyce Godber *History of Bedfordshire*, is good on the costs of enclosure.

21 Alan Cirket, *Samuel Whitbread's Notebooks, 1810–11, 1813–15*, BHRS, Vol. 50.

22 Annual Obituary of 1817; Bernard Cashman, *Private Charity and the Public Purse: The development of the General Hospital 1794–1988*, North Bedfordshire Health Authority, 1988.

23 Joyce Godber, *History of Oakley Hunt*, BHRS, Vol. XLIV, 1965.

24 William Prinsep's diary (Southill VSB 5), kindly provided by Mrs Diana Macleod.

25 Fulford, *Samuel Whitbread*, p.93; Grey letters at Durham.

26 Fulford, *Samuel Whitbread*, pp.92–6. Peter Wright's accounts at the back of Fulford's book pp. 309 ff.

27 Fulford, *Samuel Whitbread*, pp.276–96.

28 BLARS ref. W 1/ Sheridan Letters. The Gainsborough picture of his daughters is reproduced on p.15 of S. Deuchar's *Painting, Politics and Porter*. There are notes on the picture at Southill.

29 Fulford, *Samuel Whitbread*, pp.287–96.

30 ibid pp.297–308.

31 Tributes of the public press to the late Mr Samuel Whitbread, Whitbread Archive box 1 in Southill Muniment Room..

32 Fulford, *Samuel Whitbread*, p. viii.

Chapter 4 William Henry Whitbread (1794–1867) and Samuel Charles Whitbread (1799–1879)

1 Roger Fulford, *Samuel Whitbread (1764–1815): A Study in Opposition*, Macmillan, 1967, p.70. This harsh comment should be contrasted with the widespread praise in his Obituaries in 1867. He had a number of prominent artists among his friends.

2 Letter of 5 May 1805, BLARS, ref. W 1/2188.

3 William Prinsep's Diary, VSB 5.

4 Fulford, *Samuel Whitbread,* p.305; Notes on Pictures Index, Southill Muniment Room; yet letter from Judith Whitbread at Southill of 7 January 1835: 'We have a house full of people.'

5 Notes on Pictures, Southill Muniment Room

6 *Northamptonshire Mercury* for elections, especially 17 January 1835.

7 Proclamation of Queen, see *Bedford Mercury,* 24 June 1837.

8 *Huntingdon, Bedford and Peterborough Gazette* of 28 February 1829: 'On Thursday se'nnight that truly patriotic gentleman William Henry Whitbread Esq. M.P. favoured his tenants and neighbours with a day's coursing on his manor.'

9 Bernard Cashman, *Private Charity and the Public Purse: The Development of the General Hospital 1794–1988,* North Bedfordshire Health Authority, 1988, pp.109–26, 134, 144.

10 Bernard Cashman, *A Proper House; Bedford Lunatic Asylum 1812–1860,* North Bedfordshire Health Authority 1992; Archives of Bedford Lunatic Asylum and Three Counties/ Fairfield (BLARS refs. LB & LF respectively.); For English Agricultural Society see Southill Muniment Room Archive Box 45.

11 Martin Lawrence article in P. L. Bell ed. *Southill Estate, 1795–1995,* S. C. Whitbread, 1994

12 L. G. Cockman, *Railway Age in Bedfordshire*, BHRS Vol.53.

13 BLARS, ref. Z575.

14 Letter of Thomas Creevey of 6 May 1823 in Rt Hon Sir Herbert Maxwell's edition of *The Creevey Papers*, p. 413, John Murray, 1923, p.413.

15 *DNB*

16 Humphrey Whitbread Archive, W/H 3/5 January 1838.

17 Judith Whitbread, letter of 13 October 1831 relating to events of Wednesday 5 October.

18 Judith Whitbread, letter of 1 October 1834.

19 Waldegrave letters at Chewton (photocopies at Southill Muniment Room), ref. W/H 18/32-35.

20 Guide to Glenarm.

21 *Bedfordshire Mercury,* 10 February 1862.

22 *Bedfordshire Mercury* ref. to Beds Working Men Institute's visit in 1865.

23 *Bedfordshire Mercury,* 2 July 1867, W. H. Whitbread's obituary.

24 Nick Redman, 'Whitbread & Co, 1796–1889: the Period of Partnerships', *The Brewer*, April 1992.

25 For S.C Whitbread's career as MP for Middlesex see obituary of 31 May 1879, *Bedfordshire Times* which quotes from *The Examiner.*

26 BLARS ref. W3461.

27 Redman, 'Whitbread & Co, 1796–1889'.

28 *Queen*, 1 January 1916 [on the death of their son Samuel Whitbread III] (see Scrapbook in the Southill Muniment Room).

29 Humphrey Whitbread Archive ref. W4/4. Notes on the Oakley Hunt. Manuscript 1876, typed copy made, January 1916; Joyce Godber *Oakley Hunt*; W/H 4/1 Correspondence with Berkeley.

30 Andrew Francis Richer, *Bedfordshire Police 1840–1890*, Paul Hooley, 1990.

31. Gertrude Lyster, *A Family Chronicle*, (derived from notes selected by Barbara Hon. Lady Grey), Murray 1908.

32. Volumes of Meterological Observations at the Observatory, Cardington, 1848–80, Humphrey Whitbread Archive W/H 31/1-3. *The Dines Dynasty: a family of meteorologists*, proceedings of a conference of the Royal Meterological Society for the History of Meteorology & Physical Oceanography, 23 October

1993 (Copy Southill Muniment Room, VSB 6, No 12); Description of Samuel Charles Whitbread's Observatory at Cardington, 12 November 1850, Humphrey Whitbread Archive W/H 4/2.

33 *Bedfordshire Times* Obituary, 31 May 1879.

34 Hillier Sermon reported in *Bedfordshire Times,* 6 June 1879.

Chapter 5 Samuel Whitbread III (1830–1915)

1 Humphrey Whitbread Archive, WH 7/4.

2 *Bedfordshire Times* and *Bedfordshire Mercury,* 1852–1895.

3 Photocopy of Letter offering post from Palmerston, dated 17 June 1859 Humphrey Whitbread Archive W/H 6/2; Sir Algernon West *Recollections,* Smith, Elder & Co, 1899, Vol. 1 pp.269–70, useful for Whitbread's time in this post.

4 S. A. Whitbread, *Silent Hills,* Hutchinson, undated p.21. Although the book is definitely by Samuel Howard Whitbread, the publishers got his second initial wrong on the title page!

5 *Guide & Notes on history of Loch Assynt,* Southill Muniment Room VSB 5, item 3.

6 *Bedfordshire Times* and *Mercury* and *Annual Register* for 1878.

7 Obituaries of Samuel Whitbread III, copy at BLARS.

8 e.g. when Whitbread refused Presidency of Board of Trade in 1880. See Lord Morley *Recollections*, Vol. 1, Macmillan, p. 168.

9 J. V. Beckett, *The Aristocracy in England, 1660–1914*, Basil Blackwell, Oxford, 1986. p.120, discusses ennoblement of brewers.

10 BLARS ref. W 3956.

11 J. Godber, *History of the Harpur Trust*, 1552–1973, 1973; David Bushby Elementary Education in Bedford 1868–1903, BHRS, Vol. 54.

12 *Bedfordshire Times,* 2 July 1892.

13 Bernard Cashman, *Private Charity and the Public Purse: The Development of the General Hospital 1794–1988*, North Bedfordshire Health Authority, 1988.

14 Extracts from red book *House at Southill: New and Alterations made;* BLARS, ref. W3976 Analysis of cost of new Cottages built on Southill Estate for the Whitbreads in 1911. For Cardington Church see Christopher Pickford, *Bedfordshire Churches in the Nineteenth Century, I*, BHRS, Vol. 73. A brief account of the restoration of Elstow church, 1880–2 is given in Rachel Marchbank's recent *Elstow Abbey*. For a description of Southill Church, as it was in W .H. Whitbread's day, dated 1848, see Christopher Pickford, *Bedfordshire Churches III*, BHRS, Vol. 79.

15 Various obituaries of Samuel Whitbread III, copy at BLARS.

16 Southill Game Books.

17 B. Ritchie, *An Uncommon Brewer: the Story of Whitbread, 1742–1992*, James and James 1992

18 *Bedfordshire Times*, 2 July 1892: Letter of W. E. Gladstone, 24 June 1892.

19 May–June 1894.

20 Bedfordshire Times, 13 June 1896.

21 Humphrey Whitbread Archive WH 33/12 & 13.

22 Obituaries of Samuel Whitbread III., copy at BLARS.

Chapter 6   Samuel Howard Whitbread (1858–1944)

1 Though christened Samuel Howard, he was always known as Howard, to avoid confusion with his father.

2 Humphrey Whitbread Archive, W/H 8/25. Obituary probably from *(London) Times* of *S.H.* Whitbread, 1936.

3 In the Southill Library *Lord Macaulay's* Memoirs *8 Vols.* ed. Lady Trevelyan, (his sister), 1866 Edition. An album of photographs of himself and his contemporaries at Eton is held at Southill.

4   See Note 2.above: 'in 1880 he became private secretary to Lord Northbrook, who was then First Lord of the Admiralty, but politics as a career never really attracted him.'

5   His travel diary is in the Humphrey Whitbread Archive, W/H32/3. S. A Whitbread, *The Silent Hills,* Hutchinson, undated. See Chapter 5 Note 4.

6   Travel Diary part of W/H 32/1.

7   Letter of 5 November from George Melly to Sam Whitbread III: *Nugent & HW will cart round with the Papal Bull and see all the priests. Frankly it is all no use if the H* [ome] *R* [ulers] *go round as one man & vote Tory. The fanatics are sulky but few.* See also *Bedfordshire Times* of 5 December 1885. BLARS, ref W 3959,

8   Edward George Bulwer-Lytton, *Richelieu.*

9   Travel Diaries, Humphrey Whitbread Archive, W/H 32/1 & 4.

10 See *Bedfordshire Times*, September 1892 for an account of the election campaign in South Bedfordshire.

11 Sir Philip Magnus, *Gladstone*, John Murray, 1963.

12 *Bedfordshire Times,* 24 September 1892.

13 *Bedfordshire Mercury,* 1 April 1893.

14 W/H 8/1-4, 7, the Correspondence with Dunne including 8/1 which lists Howard's specific agreements over the Temperance issue with Liberals in South Beds and Bedford, 1893–1894.

15 W/H 8/5 & 6.

16 Accounts of Campaign in local newspapers.

17 Travel Diaries, W/H 32/5-8.

18 Burke's Peerage, any contemporary edition. The letters are in the Humphrey Whitbread Archive, W/H 74-77. For additional information, including Photographs, see W/H 77-78.

19 M. Whitbread, *Miss Madeline* p.51

20 Local Bedfordshire newspapers on South Huntingdonshire Campaign.

21 Madeline Whitbread's Diary; Humphrey Whitbread Archive, W/H 33/12 *Bedfordshire Times* for April & May 1908.

22 Madeline Whitbread's Diaries, 1908–14.

23 *Bedfordshire Times,* 5 June 1936. For his resignation from being Chairman of Quarter Sessions, see *Bedfordshire Times,* 8 January 1915.

24 ibid.

25 Whitbread, *Silent Hills.*

26 Folder re: S.H. Whitbread and the Society for the Preservation of the Wild Fauna of the Empire, now Fauna and Flora International. It includes sheet listing Howard's involvement 1903-7. Papers 1903-28 incl. Parliamentary question Dec. 1906 and article by S.H.W. on early days of the Society. Whitbread Archive Box 1. item 10.

27 Travel Diary, Humphrey Whitbread Archive, W/H 32/11.

28 Whitbread, *Silent Hills*, p. 146.

29 Humphrey Whitbread Archive, W/H 33/5-19 Madeline Whitbread's Diaries 1902–1936.

30 Miss Hillson's *Memories*, Southill Muniment Room.

31 W/H 8/23 *Advice on how Southill can be continued after his death*, written by Samuel Howard Whitbread for Samuel Charles.

32 *Bedfordshire Times*, 16 May 1930.

Chapter 7   Simon Whitbread (1904–1986)

1 John Pickford, *Fourth of our Magnificent Seven Series; Why the Queen's Representative is worried,* c1976 Southill Muniment Room VSB 4.

2 ibid.

3 W/H 33/15.

4 Family anecdote.

5 Humphrey Whitbread Archive, W/H 35/2 General St Aubyn to George
Burroughes, Madeline Whitbread Letters 13 November 1918; W/H 52/8.
Photograph of Stephen in Humphrey Whitbread Archive.

6 Humphrey Whitbread Archive, W/H 33/18, Madeline Whitbread's Diary.

7 Letter of Major Desmond Buxton, 15 September 1985, gives good picture of
Simon on manoeuvres in hills near Lucknow, Southill Muniment Room Archive
Box 48.

8 Madeline's Diary, Humphrey Whitbread Archive, W/H 35/21. John Pickford,
Fourth of our Magnificent Seven Series; Why Queen's Representative is worried, c1976
Southill Muniment Room VSB 4

9 Madeline's Letters, 1 March 1936, Humphrey Whitbread Archive, W/H 35/21.

10 Madeline's Diary, Humphrey Whitbread Archive, W/H 33/19.

11 Southill Muniment Room Archive Box 46.

12 John Pickford, *Fourth of our Magnificent Seven Series; Why the Queen's Representative
is worried*, Southill Muniment Room, VSB4.

13 Madeline Whitbread's letters, 9 July 1943, Humphrey Whitbread Archive, W/H
35/31

14 Madeline Whitbread's Letters, 15 December 1943; Humphrey Whitbread
Archive, W/H 35/31

15 Madeline Whitbread Letters, 19 April 1944, Humphrey Whitbread Archive,
W/H 35/32.

16 Letter, 4 March 1944, Southill Muniment Room Archive Box 46.

17 Madeline Whitbread's Letters, 19 March 1944, Humphrey Whitbread Archive,
W/H 35/32

18 John Pickford, *Fourth of our Magnificent Seven Series.*

19 Bernard Cashman, *Private Charity and the Public Purse; The development of the General Hospital 1794–1988*, North Bedfordshire Health Authority, 1988. *Bedford Group of Hospitals Survey 1948–1958,* Copy at BLARS. See especially Foreword by Simon Whitbread, Chairman.

20 *Bedfordshire Times* reporting meeting of 27 April 1962.

21 ibid., 21 April 1967.

22 ibid., 28 July 1967.

23 ibid., 12 November 1968.

24 BLARS ref. CM 14. Bedfordshire County Council Minutes.

25 *Bedford Group of Hospitals Survey 1948–1958.*

26 This comes out very clearly in his foreword to *Bedford Group of Hospitals Survey 1948–1958.*

27 Photographs, Humphrey Whitbread Archive W/H 56/3-15.

28 *Bedfordshire Times,* 1 June 1962.

INDEX

All place-names except those in Bedfordshire include the county.

Addington, Henry 33
Adeane, Charles 78
Adkin, Thomas 27, 38
Alleyn, William 4
Angus, Michael 120
Antonie, William Lee 38
Arlesey, Three Counties Lunatic Asylum
    48
Asquith, H. H. 78, 79
Assynt Lodge (Sutherland) 62, 74,
    81–82
    see also Loch Assynt

Barnard, Thomas 62, 83
BEDFORD
    gaol 23
    Group Hospital Management
        Committee 101–10
    Infirmary/County Hospital 37, 47–48,
        58, 66, 99
    Rye Close 66
    St John's hospital and church 6
    St Mary 37
    Working Men's Institute 52
    see also Bunyan Meeting (Bedford)
Bedfordshire Agricultural Society 37
Bedwell Park (Herts.) 17, 18, 24, 29
Bennett, Alex 115, 118
Berkeley, Grantley 57–58
Biddenham 13
Biggleswade, Whitbread well 67

Birley, Oswald 80
Bisgrave, Thomas 13
Bland, Michael 49
Blaunpain, family of 1
    Roger 1
Boteler, William 8
Boulton, Matthew 22
Boulton & Watt 16, 28
Bowes Lyon, Michael 109
Bradley, William, painter, 54 (ill.)
Brewers, Worshipful Company of; see
    London, Worshipful Company of
    Brewers
Brroughes, George 109
Brown, Timothy 39
Bunyan, John 5, 6
Bunyan Meeting (Bedford) 10, 13, 14,
    31
Burroughs, Stephen 94–95
Byng, John: see under Torrington
Byron, Norah 110

Caldecott, Andrew 118
Cardington 3, 4, 5, 6, 8, 9, 10, 18, 22,
    29–30, 36, 37, 47, 48, 51–52, 58,
    87, 106
    church 1, 67
    Coursing Club 47
    Great Farm (also Maltings Farm) 4, 9,
        13
    Howard's House 58

Little Farm 4
Catherwood, Mr 23
Chantrey, Sir Francis, sculptor, 50
Churchill, Winston 83, 108
Civil War 4, 5, 6, 9
Clarkson, John 19
    Thomas 19
Cleveland, Thomas Earl of 4
Collier, John 70
Colman, Tim 118
Cornwallis, Lord 20
Coxe, William 28
Creevey, Thomas 49
Croxton (Cambs.) 6

Delafield, Joseph 16, 17, 23
Dines, Charles 55, 58
Dolben, Sir William 21
Duberly, James 57

Edwards, Oliver 11, 14
Egar, Mark 118, 119
Elstow 19, 37, 67
Emmerson, Thomas, citizen and brewer
    of London 3

Farrington, Robin 118
Fenlake Barns 18
Findlay, Martin 118
Fisher, Thomas, artist x (Ion House ill.)
Fletcher-Watson, James 123
Fox, Charles James 28, 33, 34, 36

Gainsborough, Thomas, painter 17, 26
    (ill.)
Giffard/Gifford, John 6, 7
    see also Independent Congregation
Gilpin, Sawrey 38
Gladstone, W. E. 63, 64, 68–69, 74,
    75, 76
Glenarm Castle (Ireland) 51
Goodwyn's Red Lion brewhouse; see
    London, Red Lion brewhouse
Grant, Sir Francis, painter 44 (ill.)
Gravenhurst, Upper and Lower 1, 3
    Ion 1, 2, 3, 4, 9, 106
    Ion House x (ill.)
Grenville, Lord 33
Grey, Charles 27, 28, 29, 33, 34, 38, 39
    Elizabeth (see under Whitbread,
    Elizabeth)
    Sir George 61

Halliday, Edward, painter 92 (ill.)
Harcourt, Thomas, Jesuit, 3
Harpur Trust 65, 66, 70
Harvey family (of Norwich) 18
Hastings, Stephen 114, 115, 117
Hatch, Emma 77, 78
Hay, Pamela 109
Hillier, Revd. Edward 59
Holland, Henry, architect 36, 39, 123
Holland, Lord 33
Howard, John 8
Howard, John (prison reformer) 8, 22,
    23, 24, 116

Inchnadamph (Scotland) 81
Independent Congregation 6, 7, 8
Ion: see under Gravenhurst, Upper and
    Lower
Ireland 51
Isitt, Sam 99
Ive, John 9
Jennings, David 17

Keens, Sir Thomas 81
Kent, Henry Earl of 4
Kenyon-Slaney, Robin 113
Killilan (Ross-shire) 62
King's Head brewery see London,
    Chiswell Street, King's Head brewery

Lambton, William 27
Lancaster, Joseph 31
Land Tax 9
Landseer, Sir Edwin, painter 50
Lennox-Boyd, Alan 114
Letterewe (Wester Ross) 103, 110, 117
Lilburne, James 37
    Thomas 37
Lindsay, Norah 109
Little Sodbury (Glos.) 11
Local Government Act 64
Loch Assynt (Sutherland) 62
    see also Assynt Lodge
LONDON
    Bricklayers' Company 19
    Chiswell Street, King's Head brewery
        15, 16, 49, 56, 68
    Dover Street 41

Drury Lane Theatre 39–41
Middlesex Hospital 24, 102
Portman Square 17, 21
Red Lion brewhouse 16
St George's Sqaure, Pimlico 56, 68
Worshipful Company of Brewers 3,
    14 (Masters of see under Wightman,
    John)
Loughton (Buckinghamshire) 6
Luke, Sir Oliver 5
Sir Samuel 5, 6

Macan, Caroline 51
    Harriet see under Whitbread, Harriet
        (née Sneyd)
    Henry 51
    Jane 51
    (General) Turner 51
    Turner 51
McCulloch, Andrew 113
Markham, Sir Frank 100
Martineau, John 49; Joseph 49
Massey/Maysey, Broughton 17
Melville, Henry Dundas, 1st Viscount
    31–33
Molloy, Simon 118
Monoux, Sir Humphrey 8
Morley, Sam 64
Munton, Revd. Anthony 13–14

Newport Pagnell (Buckinghamshire)
    5, 6, 9
North, Lord 20–21
Northbrook, Lord 74

Oakley Hunt 38, 47, 57–58
Oates, Titus 3
Old Warden 19
Opie, Amelia 38
  John 38
Ossulston, Lord 41

Parnell, Charles 75
'Peter Pindar' 16
Phillips, J. 17
Pinckney, Captain 5, 6
Pitt, William (Earl of Chatham) 21
  William (the Younger) 30, 33
Polwarth, Lord 19
Poor Laws 30–31, 47
Portland, Duke of 19
Prinsep, William 38
Pym, Guy 68, 77

Railways 48–49
Read, Philip 11
Rennie, John 28
Reynolds, Sir Joshua, painter 12 (ill.)
Reynolds, S. W. 38
Richmond, George 60
Robinson, John 70
Romilly, Sir Samuel 41
Russell, Lord Edward 8

Sackville-West, Diana 95
St John, Lady 40
Salmon, Nicholas 45
Sandys, Colonel 75
Sangster, Robert 17, 39

Savage, Sir Thomas 4
Seymour, Raymond 118
Shaw-Lefevre, Charles 49–50
  Emma Laura (née Whitbread, younger
    sister of William Henry and Samuel
    Charles Whitbread) 50
Sheridan, Esther 39
  Richard Brinsley 28, 39, 40
Shewell, Godfrey 14, 15
  Thomas 14, 15
Shillington 2, 36, 106
ship money 4
Slater, William 17
Southill 13, 17, 19, 36–53, 55, 56, 61–
    67, 70, 71, 82, 84, 86–89, 95, 96, 99,
    102–104, 106, 108–109, 113–114,
    118–119, 122–123, 124
  Gastlings Lodge 51
Spencer, Margaret 95
Steyning (Sussex) 21

Tidbury, Charles 115, 117, 118
Torrington, George, 4th Viscount 19
  John (the diarist), 5th Viscount 22–23
Trotter, Alexander 32
Troughton, Dick 118
Turner, J. M. W., painter 50, 51

Wage Regulation Bills 30
Watt, Fiddes, painter 72 (ill.)
Weir, John 40
West Thurrock (Essex) 18–19

WHITBREAD FAMILY
arms of ii, 6
and brewing industry 3, 11, 13, 14, 15,
16, 17–19, 28, 38–39, 49–50, 55, 56,
58, 67–68, 73, 75, 76, 84, 88, 102,
115, 116, 117–118, 119–121
and Civil War 5, 9
genealogy ix, 2
origins 1–2
philanthropy 22–23, 24, 37, 51–53, 66,
106
politics 8, 10, 13, 19, 20, 21, 22, 23,
29, 30, 31–33, 46–47, 55, 61–64,
68–70, 73, 74–80, 90, 114 (and Tory
party 8, 20, 23, 29, 114–115; and
Whig party 10, 21, 29, 33–36)
portraits 12, 26, 44, 54, 60, 70, 72, 80,
89, 92, 107
religion 6, 7, 8 10, 46–47, 86–88
residences x (ill.), 2–3, 6, 9, 13, 17,
18, 19, 20, 29, 36–37, 38, 39, 40, 41,
45, 58, 66–67, 73, 74–77, 78–80,
86–90, 99, 104, 106, 108–109, 113–
114, 118–119, 122–123
see also individual family members
Whitbread, Bill 102, 103, 110, 115
Whitbread, Charles (1928–93) 115, 118
Whitbread, Charles Edward Samuel
(1963–) 122, 124
Whitbread, Elizabeth (wife of William
Whitbread 1571–1639) 3
Whitbread, Elizabeth (née Read), 2nd
wife of Henry Whitbread 1664–1727
11, 13, 14

Whitbread, Elizabeth (née Grey), wife
of Samuel Whitbread II 29, 38, 40,
46, 50
Whitbread, Elizabeth, daughter of
Samuel Whitbread II and wife of
William 8th Earl Waldegrave 45, 46
Whitbread, (Miss) Elizabeth (1829–
1913) 52
Whitbread, Francis Pelham (Frank) 61
Whitbread, (Miss) Gertrude (1826–
1909), wife of Charles James Conway
Mills 52
Whitbread, Harriet (née Sneyd), 2nd
wife of William Henry Whitbread
d.1867 and 1st wife of General
Turner Macan 51, 52, 53
Whitbread, Harriot (née Hayton), 1st
wife of Samuel Whitbread I 17, 27
Whitbread (later Gordon), Harriot,
daughter of Samuel Whitbread I 15,
18, 21, 23
Whitbread, Helen (née Trefusis) (1917–
2006), wife of Simon Whitbread
d.1985 96, 98, 99, 102–104
Whitbread, Henry (1601–1656) 2, 3,
4, 5, 6, 9
Whitbread, Henry (1664–1727) 2, 3, 9,
10, 11, 13, 18
Whitbread, Henry, son of Henry d.1727
13
Whitbread, Henry William (Harry) 61
Whitbread, Humphrey (1912–2000) 74,
97, 103, 112, 115, 123
Whitbread, Lady Isabella (née Pelham),

wife of Samuel Whitbread III 61, 70

Whitbread, Ive 9, 11, 14

Whitbread, Jane (née Hayter), wife of
Samuel Charles (Sam) Whitbread
103, 113, 118, 119, 121, 122, 124

Whitbread, John 9, 11, 13

Whitbread, Joscelyne (1906–1936)
96,103

Whitbread, Judith (née Pigott), 1st wife
of William Henry Whitbread d.1867
45, 50–51, 52

Whitbread, Julia (née Brand), 1st wife
of Samuel Charles Whitbread d.1879
56, 58

Whitbread, Juliana, wife of Thomas
Coke, 2nd Earl of Leicester 56

Whitbread, Lawrence 2

Whitbread, Lettice (née Leeds) 6, 8, 9

Whitbread, Liz (later Bennett) 109

Whitbread, Madeline (née Bourke)
(1878–1961), wife of Samuel
Howard Whitbread d.1944 74, 77–
80, 83, 84–86, 88, 89, 109–110

Whitbread, Martha 8

Whitbread, Lady Mary, widow of
Henry Stephenson and 2nd wife of
Samuel Charles Whitbread d.1879 56

Whitbread, Maud (1859–1898) 61

Whitbread, Rachel (wife of Oliver
Edwards) 11, 14

Whitbread, Samuel, I (1720–1796) 1, 9,
11, 12–24, 27, 28, 29, 30, 37, 39, 42,
88, 90, 102, 106
apprenticeship 14

and brewing 14–19

character 22, 24

death 20, 24

education 13–14

faith 24

letters to son 17–18

marriages 17

philanthropy 22–23, 24, 37

politics 20, 21

portrait 12, 107

residences 17, 18, 19, 20, 21

and slave trade 21

will 24

Whitbread, Samuel, II (1764–1815)
17–18, 19, 20, 21, 24, 26–42, 45,
46, 47, 50, 55, 58, 59, 61, 63, 73, 89,
104–105

and Bedfordshire 37–38

and brewing 28, 38–39

character 41–42

death 27, 41, 46

and Drury Lane Theatre 39–41

education 27

and enclosures 37

faith 31

and field sports 37–38

and impeachment of Lord Melville
31–33

marriage 29

politics 21, 29, 30, 33–36

and Poor Laws 30–31

portrait 26

and Princess Caroline 35

and Regency Bill 35

residences 29, 36–37, 38, 39, 40, 41, 46

and slave trade 21–22, 30

travels 28, 29

Whitbread, Samuel, III (1830–1915) 59, 60–71, 74, 77, 85

and Bedfordshire 65

and brewing 67–68

character 68–69

Civil Lord of Admiralty 62

death 71

education 61

and field sports 62, 67, 70

health 62, 70

and local government 64–65

marriage 61

and peerage 64

philanthropy 66, 67

politics 61–65, 68–70

portraits 60, 70

and Scotland 62

Whitbread, Samuel Charles (1796–1879) 38, 45, 46, 49, 54–59, 61, 89

and Bedfordshire 58

and brewing 49, 55, 56

character 59; death 58–59

description 56

duel 57–58

education 45, 55

and field sports 47, 55, 57

marriages 56

politics 55

portrait 54

residences 45, 58

scientist 55, 58

Whitbread, Samuel Charles (Sam) (1937–) 86, 96, 103, 104, 107, 108–124

and Bedfordshire 114, 115, 116, 121, 124

and brewing 115–116, 117–118, 119–121

education 109–113

and field sports 110, 112

marriage 103, 113

military service 111–112

and painting 123, 124

and photography and film 110–111

politics 114–117

residences 104, 108, 113–114, 118–119, 122–123

and Scotland 110

Whitbread, Samuel Howard (Howard) (1858–1944) 61, 62, 66, 72–90, 96, 103, 104, 106, 114, 116, 123

and Bedfordshire 80

and brewing 73, 75, 76, 84, 88

character 80, 84–85, 89–90

death 89, 98

education 73, 74

faith 86–88

and field sports 81–85

marriage 78

politics 73, 74–77, 78–80, 90

portraits 72, 80, 89

residences 86–89

travels 74, 75, 76, 77, 78, 81, 82, 83, 84

Whitbread, Sarah (née Ive) 9, 10

Whitbread, Simon (1904–1985) 74, 92–105, 108, 113, 114, 19, 117
   and Bedfordshire 99–102, 104
   and brewing 102
   character 104–105, 117
   death 104
   education 93–95, 99
   and field sports 95–96, 103
   marriage 96
   military service 93, 95, 96–99
   politics 104
   portrait 92
   residences 96, 99–104

Whitbread, William (1571–1639) 3

Whitbread, William (b.1612) 6

Whitbread, William (c 1626–1701) 6, 7, 8, 9, 10

Whitbread, William Henry (1795–1867) 31, 38, 44–53, 55, 57, 61
   and Bedfordshire 47–48
   and brewing 49–50, 67
   character 45, 52–53
   education 45, 46
   and field sports 47, 57
   marriages 46, 51, 52
   philanthropy 51–53
   politics 46–47, 52
   portrait 44
   and railways 48–49
   residences 45, 85

Wightman, John (Master of the Worshipful Company of Brewers) 14

Wilberforce, William 41

Wilkes, John 20

Wilkie, Sir David, painter 50

Williams, Rhys 83

Wilshere, William 40

Wilstead 37

Wollaston (Northamptonshire) 14

Woolmers Park (Hertfordshire) 29, 36, 45

Yallowley, Jacob 17, 39

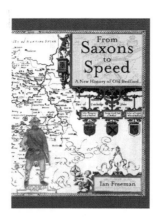

FROM SAXONS TO SPEED
A New History of Old Bedford

Ian Freeman

The early history of Bedford town has been treated in a somewhat perfunctory way by previous local historians. This is understandable because information from the "Dark Ages" is sparse whereas there is a plethora of information readily available from later centuries.

This book is an attempt to fill that gap, using what firm information there is, supplemented by intelligent speculation when necessary. As a result, a number of generally accepted "facts" are put into question, and, in some cases, shown to be wrong.

The book begins with the Saxon period through the times of King Offa and King Alfred when the settlement and basic structure of the town was being laid out. It goes on to the Norman and Platagenet periods and describes how those invaders and rulers left their mark on the town.

Finally, it looks at the town as depicted in John Speed's map of the town which he published in 1610. It describes those streets and buildings which have survived from that time and discusses some of the prominent people who have lived in the town from time to time.

THREADS OF TIME

Shela Porter

A pale-faced city child is evacuated from London during the Zeppelin raids of 1917. In Hitchin she takes a dressmaking apprenticeship and opens her own workshop with customers including the local gentry and the young Flora Robson. Moving to Bedford on her marriage, her sewing skills help her rapidly growing family to survive the Depression; working long hours during the exigencies of war-time Britain, it is her re-designed battle-jacket that Glenn Miller is wearing when he disappears over the Channel in 1944, and entertainers Bing Crosby and Bob Hope leave comics and candy for her 'cute kids'. For five years after the war the family run a small café in the town but sewing then sees her through again as the business is sold, she is widowed with a nine-year-old son to raise, all her children gradually leave and she moves away to be wardrobe mistress to a big operatic society in High Wycombe. Finally she settles in a small cottage opposite the great airship sheds at Cardington from where she once watched the ill-fated R101 take off on its last journey in 1930.

A mirror of her times, this gripping biography tells the story of a remarkable lady, a talented dressmaker, mostly in Hitchin and Bedford – played out against the unfolding drama of the entire twentieth century.

JOURNEYS INTO BEDFORDSHIRE

ANTHONY MACKAY

THE MARQUESS OF TAVISTOCK

JOURNEYS INTO BEDFORDSHIRE

Anthony Mackay

This book of ink drawings reveals an intriguing historic heritage and captures the spirit of England's rural heartland, ranging widely over cottages and stately homes, over bridges, churches and mills, over sandy woods, chalk downs and watery river valleys.

Every corner of Bedfordshire has been explored in the search for material, and, although the choice of subjects is essentially a personal one, the resulting collection represents a unique record of the environment today.

The notes and maps, which accompany the drawings, lend depth to the books, and will assist others on their own journeys around the counties.

Anthony Mackay's pen-and-ink drawings are of outstanding quality. An architectural graduate, he is equally at home depicting landscapes and buildings. The medium he uses is better able to show both depth and detail than any photograph.